How to Turn Pressure into Power

CRACKING
the STRESS
Secret

AMIR A. RASHIDIAN, DC

GREENLEAF
BOOK GROUP PRESS

This book is intended as a reference volume only, not as a medical manual. The information given here is designed to help you make informed decisions about your health. It is not intended as a substitute for any treatment that may have been prescribed by your doctor. If you suspect that you have a medical problem, you should seek competent medical help. You should not begin a new health regimen without first consulting a medical professional.

Published by Greenleaf Book Group Press
Austin, Texas
www.gbgpress.com

Distributed by Greenleaf Book Group

For ordering information or special discounts for bulk purchases, please contact Greenleaf Book Group at PO Box 91869, Austin, TX 78709, 512.891.6100.

Design and composition by Greenleaf Book Group
Cover design by Greenleaf Book Group

Publisher's Cataloging-in-Publication data is available.

Print ISBN: 978-1-62634-952-0

eBook ISBN: 978-1-62634-953-7

Part of the Tree Neutral® program, which offsets the number of trees consumed in the production and printing of this book by taking proactive steps, such as planting trees in direct proportion to the number of trees used: www.treeneutral.com

TreeNeutral®

Printed in the United States of America on acid-free paper

22 23 24 25 26 27   10 9 8 7 6 5 4 3 2 1

First Edition

Contents

Part I:
Stress, Health, and Wellness

Part II:
Ten Steps to Turn Stress into Strength
and Move toward Health and Wellness

Preface

Go confidently in the direction of your dreams!
Live the life you've imagined.

—Henry David Thoreau, *Walden*

I was nine years old when I decided that I had to become a doctor. My father wanted to show me how our ancestors had lived. So we got in the car and drove for three hours toward the mountains. Then when the road ended, we rode mules around the side of the mountain until we arrived in the village.

It was a beautiful morning.

I held my father's hand as we walked through the rural village of small, primitive mud houses nestled near the river that ran along a green mountainside. I felt the crisp fresh air as it entered my lungs. There was no smog, no power lines, and none of the telephone poles that cluttered our home city of Sari. A shepherd was tending to his flock in the distance, women were washing clothes in the river, and children were playing with sticks and stones. It felt so peaceful there.

It was as if we had gone two hundred years back in time.

The tranquil scene was broken by a frantic man screaming something in Farsi. He was panicked and distraught. Even though I spoke the same language, this man spoke in an unfamiliar dialect. Villagers rushed from everywhere to help. The desperate man led his neighbors into his home, and my father and I followed close behind. The one-room house we entered was rustic but tidy, with pots and pans stacked under a long wooden table. Large cushions lay against the wall, and an earthen floor was covered by a hand-woven red rug.

But all I could focus on was the groaning woman lying on some blankets in the corner. She was obviously pregnant and in a lot of pain. Tears rolled down her cheeks. She screamed in agony, and I grasped my father's hand tighter. Something didn't feel right about her appearance. No one knew what to do for her. So they waited and watched and suffered with her.

Finally, Zahra, the midwife, walked in. She knelt down, examined the woman for a minute or two, and then stood up. In her native tongue she said, "I'm sorry. The baby is dead, and the mother's time is short. Unless you can get her to a hospital in the next twenty minutes, she will die." With a final glance, Zahra walked out the door.

The room was silent, except for the pregnant woman's groans. One by one, the villagers left. They knew she would never survive a grueling two-hour mule ride down the mountain. They shuffled out with their heads low, not making eye contact. A look of horror covered her husband's face as he realized her death was imminent. He fell to his knees and cried in agony, kneeling and holding his arms outstretched toward the sky.

I started to cry. I actually felt pain. It was the first time in my life that an emotion was so strong that it affected me physically. It felt as if I was suffocating. I gasped for air.

Realizing my sorrow, my father, Javad, picked me up and held me close. As he carried me out of the house, he said, "Amir, my son, there was nothing that could be done. We could not help her. We have to accept that."

I nodded, but I didn't accept it. The image of that woman suffering and slowly dying while her husband sat powerless beside her was burned into my mind forever. In that moment, I could not imagine how the emotions of that day would ultimately change the entire course of my life.

Once outside, my dad and I made our way down the mountain and got in the car for the three-hour drive home.

"Amir, what is it you are thinking about?" asked my dad while driving.

"Baba, I don't want to feel that helpless ever again," I stammered, still shaken by the events of the day.

"What do you intend to do about it?"

"I'm going to become a surgeon. I will be the best surgeon in the whole world, and I will carry my bag with me everywhere I go. Baba, I'm going to save lives."

With every molecule of my nine-year-old body and pure determination, I vowed that I would do whatever it took to become the world's greatest doctor. This became my life's purpose.

Ten years later, I was a sophomore at The George Washington University in Washington, DC. I was a premedical student with stellar grades, and every aspect of my life was advancing according to my plan: to go to medical school and ultimately save lives. As fate would have it, everything was about to change!

After completing a difficult semester, I was ready for a much-needed rest. I was excited about spending Christmas break at home and seeing my parents, who had immigrated to the United States and were now living in Gaithersburg, Maryland. What I experienced as I walked through the door of the small townhouse wasn't the happy and welcoming reception that I had expected. My mom and dad didn't rush to the door with outstretched arms and warm embraces. Instead, Dad was wearing a big, thick, white neck brace and walking gingerly toward me. He was obviously heavily medicated and couldn't lift his arms to give me a hug. My mother, despite her best efforts, couldn't mask the anguish and stress that Dad's injury had caused.

"Hello! Welcome home, Son! How are you?" asked Javad, as he struggled to smile for me.

"I'm fine, Dad," I replied, but what I really wanted to say was "I can't believe you're in pain again." My father's condition was a chronic one and seemed to flare up at the most inopportune times. About ten years prior, he was involved in several back-to-back car accidents, and ever since he suffered from painful episodes, but never this badly.

I was disappointed, because I wanted to spend time with him and enjoy Christmas break. But Dad was in no condition to socialize. He was in constant pain, despite being on strong pain medicine. The excruciating pain started in his neck and shot down his arms, all the way down to his fingertips. His condition had deteriorated so much that he had no strength in his hands. He needed help with the simplest tasks like eating or getting dressed. He couldn't even lie down to go to sleep. He had to sleep in a chair, because laying his head back put too much pressure on his neck. So he sat upright, all night in a chair, in the dark, all alone.

As debilitating as the pain was, Javad's emotional stress was even worse. This was because he could no longer do what he loved. He had a passion for writing. He loved to create poems, stories, and jokes. He was an amazing storyteller and captivated his audience with his imaginative tales. Bedtime stories with Dad were my favorite memories of childhood.

My father also regularly wrote letters to local politicians, senators, and even the president. He enjoyed sharing his ideas on how the president could do his job better. Now he couldn't even hold a pen. He couldn't do what he loved doing the most, and he was depressed.

During that Christmas break, I took Dad to meet with several different doctors. Each doctor we saw referred us to another doctor. No one was offering any hope. We finally ended up at a neurosurgeon's office.

"Javad, you needed surgery a long time ago! Why didn't you come to see me sooner?" asked the surgeon, not even expecting an answer.

"I'm almost afraid to ask. What kind of surgery?" my father said.

"At this point, there isn't much else we can do. The discs in your neck have degenerated, and bone spurs are growing into the spinal canal and compressing the spinal cord," said the doctor in a monotone and unemotional voice. He sounded so confident and secure in his opinion that when he said, "Surgery is your only option," we completely believed him. He explained the procedure and asked us to call and schedule the surgery.

"Baba, do you realize how invasive this operation is going to be? He said he's going to break and remove the bones in the back of your neck and insert metal rods and screws to fuse your whole neck. You will never turn your head again, and you may not regain function of your hands."

As I was recounting the doctor's graphic description of the surgery, I started to get emotional, because the doctor had also told us there was a high risk that Dad could die while in surgery because of his age. Dad was seventy years old at the time, but the recent stresses of his life had caused him to age faster than his peers.

So we decided to get a second opinion, hoping for a better prognosis. The second neurosurgeon said exactly the same thing. As did the third surgeon.

"Go and get your affairs in order. We will operate next week," the last surgeon ordered nonchalantly.

Disappointed and discouraged, Dad and I solemnly slid into the cold back seat of the yellow taxi to go home. I sat holding the heavy stack of my father's X-rays, MRIs, and medical records. Dad was sitting next to me on the passenger side of the taxi. He grimaced with every bump that taxi hit, because each time the jolt sent a lightning bolt of pain through his entire body. It broke my heart to see my dad that way. Looking at him at that moment, I got the feeling that he was tired of living like this and that he wanted to die.

In that moment, I was transported back to the emotions I had experienced in that village ten years prior, where I saw the young woman slowly dying in her husband's arms. I felt the same helplessness that I had felt then, except this time I was watching my own father suffer. It was enough to make me second-guess my entire life's plan.

I thought, *Is this the type of news I'll have to give my patients when I'm a surgeon? Will I have to tell them that by choosing to have an operation, they could lose their life? I don't think I can do that.*

Dissecting every possible scenario in my mind, I thought, *What if we opt for the operation and he dies? What if we opt for the operation and he isn't any better afterward? What if we choose not to operate and I watch my dad suffer and slowly die?*

The internal dialogue was fueling my emotions, and I began to get choked up. My chest felt tight, I struggled to take a full breath, and my eyes filled with tears. I thought I was going to explode. This was exactly how I had felt in that village all those years ago. That was the reason I'd chosen to devote my life to becoming a surgeon.

The taxi driver noticed my father's pain.

"Sir, I see that you're in a lot of pain. I know of this chiropractor just down the street from here. I don't know what he does, but I know he helps people like you. Would you like me to take you there?"

Despondent, frustrated, and exhausted, with nothing to lose, we agreed.

When we got there, the place seemed to be under construction. We knocked and knocked until a man finally opened the door. He was a calm, relaxed man with streaks of gray in his hair. He introduced himself as a chiropractor and explained that he was in the middle of building out the suite to move his practice there.

He welcomed us in. We walked past the construction crew putting up dry wall, and since there was no place to sit, he brought out crates for us to sit on. He also brought with him a light box on which to read the MRIs and X-rays we had brought. He asked my father about his condition and how it was affecting his life. He took notes and spent what seemed to be an eternity studying the MRIs and X-rays.

With confidence, the chiropractor finally said, "I can help you. I won't do it by breaking and removing any bones from your spine, and I certainly won't insert metal rods and screws into your neck."

This sounded good so far, maybe too good.

"What I will do is perform gentle and specific chiropractic adjustments to gradually reduce tension on the spinal cord," he said, sensing my skepticism.

"You know, we just met with three of the best neurosurgeons in the country, and they all agreed that surgery is the only option. What makes you think you can help my dad?"

I spoke with a condescending tone. Concerned that the doctor would be offended, Dad firmly put his hand on my knee to remind me to be respectful.

"Your father has degenerating discs and bone spurs that are growing into the spinal canal, compressing the spinal cord. Unless we stop this process, this situation is not going to end well. I won't lie to you. It's going to be a long, hard, and potentially painful road ahead, but if you don't want surgery, this is your option. It's going to take at least six months before you notice a change in your condition, and you will need to see me six days a week during those first six months. Are you prepared to make that kind of commitment?"

I was still reluctant, but Dad was willing to try anything just to avoid the dangerous surgery, so he agreed.

That same day, after a thorough physical exam, the chiropractor gave Dad his very first chiropractic adjustment. The movement was swift and small, hardly noticeable. But the sound was crisp, loud, and clear.

Dad smiled, which was rare those days, and said, "Wow!" He lay quietly for a moment. "It feels like you just poured cold water on a hot flame. That's exactly what I needed."

By the time my father stood up after his adjustment, all his excruciating symptoms had returned, but he now had hope that over time his body could heal.

Dad faithfully went to see his chiropractor six days a week for the next six months. After the first month, he didn't think he was feeling any better, but everyone around him had noticed that he had stopped getting worse. His condition seemed to have stabilized, so he kept going.

Six months passed, and just as he had done almost every day until then, my dad walked into the chiropractor's reception room. The construction had been completed. Comfortable chairs had replaced the original primitive crates, and a beautiful granite counter separated the room from the receptionist who stood behind it. The office was very busy, and every seat held patients waiting to be seen by the doctor.

My father walked confidently up to the counter, picked up the pen, and paused as he held it in his hand. With a big smile on his face and without any assistance, he wrote his name on the sign-in sheet. To the average person this may seem insignificant, but it was the first time in over a year that he had been able to write with a pen.

Then he took that pen and held it high over his head as if lifting a trophy. He was celebrating. The patients in the reception area did not understand, but they smiled nevertheless. The receptionist behind the counter, a young woman in her late twenties with auburn hair and large brown eyes, started to cry. Every time my dad had walked into that office, she had been the one to write his name for him on the sign-in sheet. When Dad had started to gain some strength in his hands, she would hold his hand for him and try to guide it as he wrote. But each time he attempted, he would drop the pen and get frustrated. But on that day, and every day after that, my dad was able to sign in on his own. Once again, he could pursue his passion, and guess who started receiving letters from my dad all over again? Yes, the president and senators.

Dad lived another eighteen years after that. At the age of eighty-eight, he seemed younger than he was at seventy. He woke up early every morning to exercise. Then he would head out the door to visit his friends, most of whom were confined to nursing homes. He was self-sufficient and traveled regularly, both across the country and abroad. He lived a good life, enjoying every moment.

I am eternally grateful to have been in that particular taxi that important day, and we are indebted to the chiropractor who gave my father his life back. Thanks to that taxi driver and loving care of the chiropractor, my dad lived long enough to watch me graduate and become a doctor, long enough to stand next to me as my best man when I got married, and long enough to meet my first son when he was born. I am blessed beyond measure to have been able to spend an extra eighteen quality years with him, the man I respected and loved so much.

I'm sharing this story with you to explain how I found my passion for health and wellness, the story of how I discovered the profession that has the power to improve so many lives and help so many people.

This story is not intended to be an advertisement for chiropractic treatment; rather, it is meant as a call to take care of your health.

Now that you know my story, please answer this question: When my dad was sick and suffering, was he the only one who suffered? Who else was affected?

You may say that I, his son, suffered, that his whole family did, and that anyone who loved him felt some degree of pain. If that is true, the same goes for you and your family. Who else will be hurt if you allow your health to decline? Our own health should be our first priority. What my sons and my wife want from me is the same thing I wanted most from my father—to be there for them when they need me and to be around for a long time. It's all I wanted from my dad, and it's all your family wants from you.

If you take your health seriously and if you invest in your well-being, you're not doing it just for yourself. You're doing it for your kids and your parents. You're doing it for your spouse and those who love you. Keep that in mind as you apply and implement what you read in this book. Because the way you take care of your health has just as much to do with others as it does with you. And that, dear reader, is exactly why I wrote this book.

Introduction

The doctor of the future will give no medicine but will
interest his patients in the care of the human frame, in
diet, and in the cause and prevention of disease.

—Thomas Edison, "Edison Hails Era of Speed"[1]

Do you have great aspirations? Are you chasing a dream? Have you decided that you want a better life? If you have desires to grow your life, your family, your circle of influence; if you want to increase your income and your quality of life; if you desire a better-looking, healthier body; if you want to improve your athletic abilities and level of fitness, then you have probably already realized that all those things are accompanied by a level of stress that you did not anticipate, expect, or plan for. No one told you it was going to be this difficult. The obstacles are too many, and you may have wondered if you'll ever achieve your goal. You may have even uttered phrases such as the following:

I don't have what it takes.

This is too stressful.

I'm too old.

I'm too young.

Anything worth having, doing, and becoming will always come with resistance, obstacles, setbacks, and most definitely a ton of stress. How well you do, how much you accomplish, and who you become in the process are completely dependent on how much stress you can safely handle. Trying to reduce or eliminate stress is the same as turning your back on the dreams and desires of your heart.

In this book, I hand over the keys to becoming the kind of person who can handle the stresses that you will surely face on that road to building a great life. I reveal to you the secret to health, wealth, and happiness.

So if you have great aspirations, this book is for you. If you dream of a better life, if you want to start and build a business, if you want to be a more effective leader, if you want to set a positive example for your family members, this message is for you.

If, on the other hand, you have been hitting a lot of roadblocks and obstacles, or you're having a hard time breaking through a plateau, consider implementing the secrets in this book. I know too many people who keep working harder and harder but can't seem to get anywhere. They're putting in more effort, more time, and more money than ever before and just can't seem to get ahead. The answer is in how equipped you are to handle stress. If any of this describes you, you'll definitely want to read this book.

You may be someone who is feeling tremendous stress. You may be pulling long hours and burning the candle at both ends. You may be having a hard time balancing your career and professional life with your family responsibilities, and all of that is affecting your health. The stress is causing mood swings, anxiety, and depression. You have a lack of energy and motivation. You feel that your body is breaking down, falling apart, and aging too fast. This book is especially written for you.

I encourage you to journey with me as I teach you how to use stress as a natural source of fuel for success. Some of what I share with you may sound familiar, but for the most part, it will feel as if you're finding out that Earth is round for the first time. I share concepts and ideas that, at first glance, will seem counterintuitive and even a bit controversial. Keep in mind that if our present stress paradigm were accurate, there wouldn't be a health-care crisis in the world. Here are a few of those controversial ideas:

- At least 80 percent of chronic diseases are lifestyle illnesses that are preventable.[2]

- In the United States, nearly nine hundred thousand people will die every year because of lifestyle choices.[3]

- The sugar-free revolution caused a tripling of the number of people with type 2 diabetes.[4]

- The fat-free movement caused the increase in obesity and heart disease.[5]

- Obesity and heart disease are more likely a result of how you eat than what you eat.[6]

- The germ theory is incomplete and fails to describe the true cause of disease.[7]

- Stress doesn't cause illness.

You may be pondering why some people can accomplish great feats with relative ease while others struggle so much. You may be wondering why some people seem to never get sick while others are

CRACKING THE STRESS SECRET

always battling colds, the flu, sinus infections, heartburn, and head-aches. Or perhaps you are wondering whether genetics play a role in a person's level of health, wealth, and happiness—and to what extent and how we can change it.

On the other hand, you may have faced health-related frustrations such as the following: Why can't I lose weight? Why don't I sleep well? Why is my blood pressure so high? Why is my cholesterol so high? Why am I always constipated? Why are my hands and feet always cold? How do I get out of pain? I know that some of these questions resonate deeply with you. Or you might know of friends, family members, or loved ones who are struggling with one or more of these things. The information in this book is vitally important and written just for you.

Don't read this book if you don't want to change your life. Put it down right now if you plan to just read but not implement the infor-mation. Give it to someone else if you never get sick and don't worry about your health. If you look and feel younger than your age, then this book definitely isn't for you. If success comes easily to you, every goal you set succeeds, and everything you touch turns into gold, you may stop reading right now.

I know what you're thinking. You're thinking that this is just another self-help book that says the same things under a different title. You probably think that I'm just going to tell you to eat better and exercise and you'll feel better. You're skeptical about being able to overcome your life's obstacles. You have read all the other books on health and wellness, success and happiness, motivation and inspiration, and none of them have helped you. You enjoyed reading those books, and you were thoroughly entertained by them, but at the end of them, noth-ing changed. I feel for you, and I completely understand how you feel. Those thoughts are the very reason I wrote this book—not to be another version of the same old advice, but to reveal the truth.

The experts in those other books tell you to reduce stress. I show what a grave mistake that can be. Your level of health is based not on the amount of stress in your life but on exactly how much stress you can safely handle. I have been studying the human body's response to stress for over twenty years, and I can say with great certainty that the number one reason people fail to reach their desired level of health, wealth, and happiness is because their bodies are not equipped to handle the stress that accompanies those things. I demonstrate why eating right and exercising aren't enough to change how you look and why just working harder for longer hours is not going to get you to the proverbial promised land. If hard work and long hours were enough for success, more people would be more successful, do more amazing things, and have more extravagant lives.

What use is great wealth if it comes at the expense of your health? On the other hand, what use is great health if it comes at the expense of your career, your dreams, and your life's purpose? Is it possible to have it both ways? Does that sound too good to be true? Are there people who have it all? Yes, but very few. So it is possible. And, if it is possible, then what do those people have and do that the rest of us don't?

Here's the secret. Those people have a different definition of stress. They prepare in advance for the stress. They train to handle the stress. They use methods and techniques that are available to all of us, but very few people actually use them. Most importantly, they never focus on reducing stress. They work on increasing their resilience in the face of stress so that they can take the hits and keep moving forward. They can carry that burden and not have it knock them down, so they can accept all the responsibilities that they want and succeed every single time. And when stress comes their way, they invite it in and embrace it. They use it as a fuel and a springboard that propels them toward success.

As a doctor in private practice, I have realized that there are a tremendous number of misconceptions with regard to basic terms in this subject, and everyone has different personal definitions for simple concepts such as health, wellness, and stress. If I ask one hundred people to tell me the definition of health, I will probably get one hundred different answers. Most will revolve around the concept that health is equivalent to looking good and feeling good. Well, health is much more than that. In this book you will find that the true definition of health is proper function and not merely the absence of disease. You will find that wellness is the degree to which health and vitality are experienced in every dimension of life. And you will agree that the true definition of stress is that it is a force that causes change in your life. Therefore, if you want to change your life, you absolutely need stress.

However, today's doctors, "experts," and the media are constantly telling us to reduce stress. More and more, they are blaming stress for the lack of health and wellness in today's society. They blame obesity on stress. They blame their headaches, heartburn, and high blood pressure on stress. Just look at the statistics. The more we focus on reducing stress, the more our health declines. There is a crisis today, and it is called sickness. Early detection is not prevention, and stress is definitely not the problem. We need to change before time runs out. Let this book guide you to the solution for you and your family. Learn how to prepare and train to handle the stress and then use that stress to propel you toward health, happiness, and success.

I know that many experts and perhaps the media will attack me for this countercultural and controversial message. They may try to discredit the information and persuade you otherwise, but I believe it is time you learned the secrets of the ultrahealthy and the ultrasuccessful. Now is the time to take charge of your health and reclaim your life so you can pursue your dreams and serve your life's purpose.

In this book you will learn the why and the how of successfully accepting stress, so you can be, do, and have all that you want. Through my personal stories of growing up in the war-ridden country of Iran, along with real-life stories of my most memorable patients, I teach you the secret to becoming the kind of person who can handle any amount of stress on the journey toward greatness.

By the time you finish reading this book, you will have a clear understanding of what stress is and how dangerous it can be to navigate through life without the tools to manage stress properly. You will walk away with practical strategies that you can implement immediately not only to improve your physical health but also to enable you to meet the demands of your personal and professional life without sacrificing your physical and emotional well-being.

Allow me to introduce you to your Stress Monkey.

PART I

STRESS, HEALTH, AND WELLNESS

CHAPTER 1

Meet Your Stress Monkey

The amount of success you achieve in life is
directly proportionate to the amount of stress
you are willing to embrace.

—Marshall Sylver, "Turning Point" seminar

Monkeys are very cute and can act like adorable human children. However, if you ask those who have tried to keep monkeys as pets, you'll hear horror stories of how the monkey attacked and hurt its owner. Untrained monkeys will get into everything and destroy anything in their way. They will urinate and defecate on everything, including their owner. They will tear up windows, doors, walls, and wiring. What a nightmare!

On the other hand, monkeys that are trained as service animals are absolutely invaluable to their owners. They are predominantly used to assist quadriplegics who have suffered a spinal cord injury. The trained monkeys flip light switches, play DVDs, fetch objects, push buttons, open bottles and put straws in them, scratch an itch on their owner's face, help them put their arm or leg back onto the wheelchair, and turn the page on the book or magazine they're reading. They basically become the hands of those who cannot use their own hands. How amazing!

Your Stress Monkey is exactly the same. It can wreak havoc in your life and health, or it can be your greatest asset. The ten-step process in this book teaches you exactly how to tame your Stress Monkey and turn your greatest stress into your biggest asset.

The Wellness–Illness Continuum

To accomplish this, we need to begin by understanding where we are with respect to wellness and illness. Visualize yourself standing with your arms spread as far apart as possible, with your right index finger pointing to the right, your left index finger pointing to the left, and your Stress Monkey sitting on your shoulders. Assume the right index finger is pointing toward wellness and the left index finger is pointing toward illness. Let this represent the wellness continuum, and your body represents where you currently stand on that continuum.

The important thing to know is that life is never static. You are constantly moving in one of two directions. You are either moving toward wellness or away from wellness and toward illness. Every thought, action, and decision you make moves you in one of these two directions. Your daily choices and the influences of your Stress Monkey are constantly pushing you back and forth on the vast spectrum of wellness and illness. You cannot move toward wellness and illness simultaneously, just as you cannot be traveling east and west simultaneously.

We all live on that continuum between illness and health. Since we are never standing still and every choice we make moves us in only one of two directions, be brutally honest with yourself right now. In which direction are you moving? If your Stress Monkey is wreaking havoc and your daily habits, thoughts, and actions are moving you toward illness and away from wellness, then let this be your wake-up call. Let this be the moment you make a change.

Consider the insights of Dr. Russ Reiss, a well-known cardio-thoracic surgeon. In a television interview, Dr. Reiss discussed how he could usually predict which heart attack patients would recover, how quickly they would recover, and which were in danger of not surviving. He said his predictions were not dependent on how skilled the surgeon was or how well the surgery went. He said the outcome was mostly dependent on the patient's lifestyle up to the moment of having a heart attack.

If you live long enough, you will eventually be faced with a serious health challenge, Dr. Reiss said. That health challenge can be an illness, disease, or life-threatening injury. How you come out of that challenge depends on how you've been living your life up to that moment. Dr. Reiss's point was that even those who live healthy lives will likely get sick at some point in their life, but their chances of full recovery will be much higher if they have been living the wellness lifestyle.[1]

In other words, according to Dr. Reiss, your lifestyle directly affects your body's ability to overcome illness, injury, and even surgery. His message should be empowering because, although you do not have the ability to fully control when a health challenge will come your way, you do have the power to influence its outcome by making the right lifestyle choices today.

Two Health and Wellness Experts Who Got Cancer

Two doctors, whom I know and respect, were both diagnosed with cancer a few years ago. One developed breast cancer and the other developed colon cancer. They were both devastated by the news of their diagnosis. It made them question everything they had done and everything they stood for. You see, both doctors were extremely fit and healthy. They exercised and ate right. They managed their lives in balance between work and home. They regularly lectured on how to prevent diseases, such as cancer, and they followed their own advice. How could they have gotten cancer?

Well, exactly one year later, both of them were cancer-free. In fact, I sat among the audience when one of them was discussing her journey, and when she spoke about her battle with breast cancer, she sounded as if she was speaking about a simple cold or a sore throat. Imagine facing an evil giant like cancer, slaying it, and coming out on the other side talking about it as if it were nothing. That's what the healthy lifestyle is all about, and that's how taming your Stress Monkey can serve and protect you.

The lesson they learned is that doing all that they did for wellness did not make them invincible, but it did give them the fighting edge they needed to be victorious. My doctor friends didn't know it, but they had been preparing for the fight of their lives by living the wellness lifestyle. Sometimes we think the only reason we do the right things is to prevent such diseases. But the main reason to tame that Stress Monkey is to become stronger so that you can overcome such obstacles.

Are You Prepared?

Muhammad Ali once said, "The fight is won or lost far away from witnesses—behind the lines, in the gym, and out there on the road, long before I dance under the lights."[2] Sooner or later, we will all be forced to step into the ring, and our opponent may be bigger than we are. We may be facing heart disease or cancer. We may be facing stroke or multiple sclerosis. If we have been preparing and if we have been training, if our Stress Monkey is fighting on our side, then we have a chance at winning. Are you training? Are you prepared? If you haven't been doing what you need to do up to now, this book will be your starting point.

Making Choices

About a decade ago, I was about to give a lecture to a group of police officers on health and stress. Outside the building, two men were standing near the entrance. One of them was eating a bag of potato chips and drinking from a can of soda. Neither of them knew that I was their next presenter. I overheard one tell the other, "I can't believe we have to sit through another health class. They're probably just going to tell me to stop eating this junk, but I would rather enjoy my life, and if that means I will die a few years sooner, so be it."

I hear that a lot, and I know that many people feel that way. They would rather trade in a few years of life for some short-term pleasure.

That wouldn't be so bad if that's all their poor habits did. In reality, the very thing they are trying to protect, their quality of life, is the first thing that will be taken away from them. The purpose of taming your Stress Monkey isn't to merely prolong life. The purpose is to increase how well you live while you are alive.

What parameters do you use to measure your quality of life?

I recently met a woman in her sixties who was obese and diabetic. Her children and grandchildren were worried about her health. Her doctors had warned her that she was in serious danger of having a heart attack or a stroke. Her diet consisted mostly of pastries, chocolate, and ice cream. She contested, "My pastries, chocolate, and ice cream are the only joy I have left in life, and I'm not going to give them up." To be honest, there are times in my life when I choose my food purely on the basis of how much pleasure it will give me. However, I consider this to be temporary and fleeting. I believe lasting joy comes from your relationships, your travels, your participation in exciting events and activities, and your ability to do good for others.

Dr. Eric Plasker puts the choice between illness and wellness in great perspective. He is the best-selling author of *The 100-Year Lifestyle*. He states that typically when he asks people, "If you knew you'd live to one hundred, how would you change your life?" they reply that they have no desire to live that long. People don't want to live to be a hundred years old, because it is believed that most people who are that old are not healthy. They need help getting out of bed and going to the bathroom, and that quality of life isn't what most people want.[3]

So why would anyone want to live to be one hundred years old? Dr. Plasker states that one of the fastest-growing age groups is the hundred-year-olds.[4] According to the United Nations, about half a million people in the world are at least one hundred years old, and that number is expected to grow eightfold within the next thirty years.[5] The startling fact is that when they were born, over a hundred years ago, life expectancy was only fifty. That means they have outlived their life expectancy by over fifty years. What was your life expectancy when you were born? Seventy? Seventy-five? What if you outlive your life expectancy by fifty years? We may not have the desire to live to be one hundred years old, but the truth is that we don't have a choice. The only choice we get is how healthy we are when we get there.

On November 5, 2005, ABC's *Good Morning America* did a story on a man who was about to turn one hundred. His name was Dr. Frank Shearer. "Shearer, a retired physician in Washington State, might be the world's oldest water-skier," the reporter explained. "He also rides horses and can be seen atop a steed on the cover of this month's *National Geographic* magazine, which features him in an article about longevity."

"I think it has to do with the fact that I have been so active," Shearer said. "I've been active all my life, from one sport to the other sport—snow-skiing in the wintertime, water-skiing in the summertime, hunting, fishing, and especially in recent years, I've been doing some weightlifting regularly."[6]

As I said, you don't get to decide how long you live. You can only decide how well you live while you're alive. Do you want to be the one-hundred-year-old who can no longer walk, or would you rather be skiing, hunting, fishing, and lifting weights when you're one hundred years old?

If you ask most financial planners, "When is the best time to invest money?" they will likely say twenty-five years ago. Well, the best time to invest in your health would have been twenty-five years ago, too. However, the next best time to invest in your health and begin taming your Stress Monkey is right now. Financial investments have the potential of losing, but health investments never lose.

The Good Life

What does it mean to live well? It is like the definition of health. Being healthy doesn't just mean being free of pain. It means that your body is functioning optimally in all areas of life. Similarly, living well doesn't mean avoiding junk food, drugs, and alcohol. Living well is about doing amazing things in your life. It's about experiencing life to the fullest. It's about serving your family, being a blessing to others, and leaving the world a bit better than when you found it. There's no end to it. Health is not a destination, and neither is wellness. Wellness is a direction and a lifestyle.

How much do you want to accomplish in your life? How many dreams do you want to chase? How many goals do you want to reach? How many people do you want to positively influence? How successful do you want to be in your career? How strong do you want to be? How much endurance and agility do you want to have? All of those things are dependent on only one thing. They are all determined by how much stress you can handle. The more stress you can handle, the less likely you are to suffer from an illness. The more stress you can handle, the less likely you are to get depressed or suffer from anxiety. The more stress you can handle, the more likely you are to live your life to the fullest.

The people who are solely focused on reducing stress end up living a very limited life, avoiding anything that may challenge them. Your goal should never be to reduce stress. Your focus should be on increasing your adaptability to stress to decrease the probability of a negative consequence of stress. In other words, stop trying to eliminate stress, and start getting stronger so you can handle more stress.

Attempting to reduce stress is like chasing the wind. You will never catch it. The only way to reduce stress is by playing small and setting the bar low. You can easily reduce your stress by getting rid of everything that is meaningful to you. Imagine if I said having children is stressful, so I'm going to give up my three sons. Absolutely ridiculous! I love my boys, and I would die for them. Believing that reducing stress will make you healthy is the same as believing you will get stronger in the gym by lifting less weight. You get stronger only if you challenge yourself by attempting to lift more weight.

So don't waste your efforts on reducing stress. Instead, invest your time and energy into taming your Stress Monkey. The Stress Monkey has incredibly awesome powers, and when he is properly trained, he will strengthen you so you can take the hits and still keep moving forward. He will empower you to carry that burden and not have it knock you down. He will enable you to accept the challenges that you want and succeed every single time.

You see, your level of health is entirely dependent on how much stress you can handle. If your stress adaptability is low, a little bit of stress will make you sick. If it is high, then you can handle tons of stress and you won't get sick. This is what a well-trained Stress Monkey will do for you. It will make you resilient in the face of stress. It will enable you to take on the stress of caring for your family, the stress of succeeding in a long and fruitful career, the stress of building a legacy, realizing your dreams, and contributing to society. I have been studying the human body for the past twenty years, and I can tell you with great certainty that the number one reason people fail to realize their dreams is that their bodies are not equipped to handle the stress that they will surely face on the road to greatness.

Just as the strength of your health is dependent on how much stress you can handle, your level of success depends entirely on how much stress you can handle. For example, the size of your family and your circle of friends depend entirely on how much stress you can handle. The length of your career and how far you go in that career depend on how much stress you can handle. The size of your business depends entirely on how much stress you can handle. Your income depends on how much stress you can handle. How wealthy you become and how happy you are depend entirely on how much stress you are equipped to handle. Everything that is worth having, doing, and becoming is completely dependent on your ability to handle the stress that accompanies it.

So when stress comes your way, become the kind of person who invites it. Accept your Stress Monkey as an ally and use it to make you stronger when fighting life's many battles. Embrace the stress, because it is a high-octane fuel that can empower you to grow in health and excel in life. Taming your Stress Monkey is the only way you can be, do, and have all that you desire. This truly is the secret to health, wealth, and happiness.

CHAPTER 2

Stress and Health

Look deep into nature, and then
you will understand everything better.

—Albert Einstein, to his stepdaughter,
Margot Einstein, 1951

O ne night, when I was seven years old, my parents told me
that I had to sleep with the radio on. So I turned on the
radio and turned up the volume. There was no programming on this station, and the radio was silent. I quickly fell into a
deep and peaceful sleep. Then, after midnight, a loud siren blared
through the radio, and I frantically flew out of bed. With my parents,
we ran out the door, through the hallway, and down the stairs all the
way to the basement. Our neighbors from the building were already
down there. They were all huddled in groups. Some were talking quietly. Others were praying. The air was heavy with fear.

Suddenly, we heard the deafening roar of a jet engine pass overhead. The noise was so loud that the entire building vibrated. At the same time, we heard the whistle of a bomb that had just been dropped. Everybody gasped. My mother hugged me tight. The whistle got louder and louder as the bomb got closer and closer. But the sound was so high pitched that we couldn't place it. It could have been right over our heads, or it could have been two blocks away. There was no way to tell.

We were petrified, and all we could do was helplessly wait, hope, and pray. Then came the loud earthshaking boom of the explosion. The walls of the building trembled and the lights flickered. I squeezed my eyes so tightly shut that I thought they would have to be pried open. Then there was just silence. Not the silence of death, not for the people in our building anyway. We were still alive. We were safe, because the bomb had hit a building a block away. The year was 1981 and the place was Tehran, Iran, during the Iran-Iraq war.

Can you imagine how we felt hearing the screaming pitch of the bomb as it was falling through the air, not knowing if those were our last moments? *That* was a stressful night for me, and I bet my Stress Monkey was wreaking havoc on my body.

Would you agree that this type of stress, when experienced night after night, could cause a decline in your health?

Stress is relative. Pollution, recession, unemployment, foreclosures, bankruptcies, national debt, Social Security, national health-care reform, child obesity, internet pornography, new technology, education, retirement, taxes, keeping up with the Joneses—these are all stressors that affect people differently, but ultimately, they all create stress.

So what is stress? How does it affect us, and how does it affect our health?

In today's world, stress is ubiquitous and is quite often blamed for many of the chronic health problems that we face as a society. More than ever before, doctors are citing stress as the source or cause of certain disorders and are prescribing antianxiety and antidepressant medication at record rates.

Those disorders include common conditions such as the following:

- Back pain
- Acid reflux
- Fibromyalgia
- Irritable bowel syndrome
- High blood pressure
- Obesity
- Headaches

The question to ask is this: Can stress really cause health problems such as headaches? And if the answer is yes, we must then ask the more important question of why. Why would stress cause headaches? An even more important question would then be this: How can we learn to manage stress to prevent such negative health consequences?

What Is Health?

In conversations with my patients, I have realized that most people's understanding of disease and illness is based on incredibly erroneous myths about health and wellness. One such premise is that health is the absence of disease. Consider a man who is moderately overweight with only slightly elevated blood pressure, who cannot climb a set of stairs without running out of breath, does not have the strength to lift a forty-five-pound suitcase, and lacks the flexibility to bend and tie his shoelaces. This man is free of all diseases, but given the limitations listed, would you consider him to be healthy?

Would you agree, then, that being healthy is not equal to the absence of disease? Thinking about your health after you've gotten sick is like putting on your seatbelt after you've crashed your car. Does maintaining dental hygiene require you to brush and floss your teeth only when you have a painful cavity, or is it a lifetime process of daily tasks? In the same way, being healthy is a lifestyle and not merely the absence of disease.

Over 90 percent of diseases are lifestyle diseases and preventable. In fact, Dr. James Chestnut, one of the foremost experts on wellness and human physiology, states that eight out of ten people on our continent will die of lifestyle choices.[1] It is disturbing to think that eight out of every ten people we know are making choices that are slowly killing them.

Those of us who live in the United States are blessed with the fact that our country is the best in the world in urgent care. The best hospitals in the world are in America.[2] We're number one! That means, if you are planning to have a heart attack or a stroke, this is the country to do it in. Isn't that comforting? Basically, as American citizens, we can just relax with absolute peace of mind. Let's not exercise. Let's smoke, let's drink, and let's eat junk food. Let's also volunteer for field duty with the bomb squad and experience the exhilarating thrill of defusing a ticking time bomb. Let's put our trust in the urgent-care system. After all, it's the best in the world.

Although 90 percent of all diseases are preventable, they aren't being prevented.[3] We know that, because each year the numbers keep going up. In fact, between the time I began writing this book and the moment you read it, all the statistical data on disease prevalence will have changed for the worse. The United States may be number one in urgent care, but we are ranked thirty-seventh in the world at keeping our citizens healthy, according to the World Health Organization.[4] This is, in part, due to the fact that this country does not have enough health-care providers, although we have plenty of urgent-care and sick-care providers.

You see, more and more people are now dying from those preventable diseases than ever before. For the first time in history, in 2012, life expectancy decreased for some subsets of the American population.[5] In 2018, before the COVID-19 pandemic, the Centers for Disease Control and Prevention (CDC) announced that US life expectancy continues to decline today.[6] Then life expectancy dropped by another 1.5 years during the pandemic—the biggest drop since World War II, according to a report by the CDC's National Center for Health Statistics.[7] This means that our generation is not expected to live as long as the previous generation. It also means that our children will not live as long as we do. Currently, there are children and teenagers battling obesity, type 2 (adult onset) diabetes, and degenerative arthritis, all of which used to be old-age problems that did not exist in children. It is becoming so common that it is actually considered normal to put children on cholesterol medication. This was the title of an article published on WebMD on February 16, 2009: "About 200,000 U.S. Teens and Preteens Need Medication to Keep Their Cholesterol Levels in Check, Study Shows."[8] According to *Consumer Reports*, 2.8 million prescriptions were written for children for cholesterol-reducing drugs in 2009.[9] I wonder what that number is today. I fear that in this next generation, our own children will have heart attacks at the age of thirty, and it will be considered normal. What in the world is normal about a heart attack, at any age?

If that is not the kind of world you want to live in, and it is not the kind of world you want your children to grow up in, then you have to become your own health-care provider. You have to take responsibility for your own health and learn to tame your Stress Monkey. You have to be the one to determine what you do and don't do for your health. I encourage you to be proactive in managing your own health and lifestyle. In doing so, you can change the future and restore hope for your children and grandchildren. It begins right here, right now.

The Origin of Stress as a Medical Term

Does stress play a role in our health? The answer is yes, but how? The word "stress" was coined by Dr. Hans Selye. His work on stress originated from his observation of hospital patients while he was still a student in medical school. In one instance, during Grand Rounds (a teaching practice where medical students are presented with a patient's medical history and problems), one of his professors asked him what he thought the problem was with a particular patient being studied. Hans noticed that although the disease process may have been different, the patient exhibited many of the same signs and symptoms as all the other patients in the hospital. But the word "stress" had not yet been used to describe medical conditions. So when asked, "What do you think is wrong with the patient?" Hans answered by saying, "This patient looks sick." At which time, all the interns and residents present began to laugh.

Today, Dr. Selye would probably say that the patient is displaying a nonspecific response to a stressful situation. Although he was ridiculed for his answer, Dr. Selye knew he was right. He had observed similarities that were common to all patients, no matter what their illness was called.[10] Those similarities are what he later described as the stress response of the body. He went on to publish many books and groundbreaking articles on the concept of stress and how the body's response to stress, over time, can result in the following:

- Hormonal imbalance
- High blood pressure
- Arteriosclerosis
- Arthritis
- Kidney disease
- Ulcers
- Allergic reactions

His extensive research on the subject of stress proved that most sickness is the result of the body's inability to adapt to stress. Your ability to adapt to stress is determined by how well trained your Stress Monkey is.

How You Handle Stress Is a Big Factor in Your Overall Health

Why is it possible that two different people can be exposed to the same pathogen, the same virus or bacteria, and one will get sick while the other stays symptom-free? Why is it possible that a group of people can eat spoiled food in an unsanitary restaurant and most of them get food poisoning, but a select few don't? Why doesn't everyone catch a cold in the winter? If the cause is the same, each body's reaction should also be the same. If the bacteria are really the cause of the disease, then every person exposed to that type of bacteria should display the same exact symptoms, in the same exact way, every single time.

What if the truth is that those who display symptoms, those who get sick, were actually already sick? Don't just gloss over that question, but really think about it. What if we are wrong about what we define as being sick?

An experiment was once performed in which two groups of people were injected with the flu virus.[11] I'm not sure how they encouraged these people to volunteer for this study, but the results were astonishing.

The first group of subjects comprised Type A, highly driven, career-focused people. They were the type of people who could be termed workaholics. They worked very long hours, spent very little time in leisure, and rarely went on vacations. For lack of a better term, their lives were out of balance. The second group consisted of individuals who balanced their time between work and play. These people were in committed relationships and spent time with family and friends. They also made time for regular social events and were involved in organizations outside their profession.

When the first group was injected with the flu virus, the subjects were bedridden for several days. They suffered from a spectrum of symptoms, such as sinus congestion, runny nose, cough, headache, and joint aches. On the other hand, when the second group was injected with the same flu virus, in the same exact way, the individuals hardly showed any symptoms. Why is that?

I hope you're ready for the answer: The first group was already sick. This is profound, because it was their lifestyle that over time had reduced their ability to handle stress. The truth is that both groups contracted the flu, but the second group had well-trained Stress Monkeys, which rendered them able to deal with the flu much better than the first group, who had clearly neglected their Stress Monkeys and allowed them to run wild.

Have you ever wondered where the flu virus goes in the summer? Is the flu virus like a goose that likes to fly north for the summer and south for the winter? Is it like a bear that likes to hibernate, except it hibernates in the summer instead of the winter? Is it like an owl that sleeps during the day and wakes up when it's dark, except the flu virus sleeps when it's warm and wakes up only when it's cold? The fact is that the flu virus does not migrate, does not hibernate, and isn't too concerned about the weather outside. It is always present, day and night, summer and winter. Haven't you ever heard of someone catching a cold or the flu in the summer?

Think about Dr. Hans Selye's research on stress. His focus was not on the stress, but the body's response to stress. One of the stresses that we must deal with in the winter is cold weather. The human body must maintain its core temperature at 98.6 degrees, and if the outside temperature is less than that, the body is placed under stress. Therefore, the body must work to bring the core temperature up to its ideal level. The colder it gets, the harder the body must work. Therefore, cold weather is a stressor, and it is a source of stress that your Stress Monkey needs to be properly trained to deal with.

Is it not true that people handle stress differently? In some individuals, stress will cause a weakened immune system, which makes them susceptible to colds and flu. In some individuals, stress will cause a heart attack or a stroke. In others, it will cause heartburn, acid reflux, or indigestion. In some individuals, stress will cause tension headaches or migraine headaches.

It is time for a major paradigm shift in how we view health. We have to accept that the person who "catches" a cold was already sick, and their Stress Monkey was untrained and unprepared for the stress.

The person who "contracts" the flu was already sick. The one who has a heart attack was already sick. You and I may be sick already.

A highly respected colleague once used an analogy to illustrate this concept. He said that vultures do not kill animals. They show up only when the animal is already dead. In the same way, many classes of bugs, bacteria, and viruses can't really hurt people in small amounts, but they attack when the body is weak and multiply when the Stress Monkey is untamed.

An example of this would be *streptococcal* bacteria. Strep can be found in practically every human being, but not every human being currently has a sore throat or strep throat. It becomes a disease only when there is an overgrowth of the strep bacteria, and this overgrowth can occur only if the body is weak and allows it to happen.

Another similar example would be *Candida albicans*, which causes yeast infections. These microorganisms are always present, but an overgrowth will cause sickness just as an overgrowth of fungus in the body would cause an infection.

I am not stating that the old concept of the germ theory is incorrect. I am just pointing out that it is incomplete and outdated. It fails to explain why the same germ (bacteria/pathogen) does not cause the same exact symptoms in every human body in the same exact way and according to the same exact timeline.

For the germ theory to be considered an irrefutable law, the germ should cause the same illness, in the same way, every single time. The majority of the common pathogens and germs are very opportunistic in nature and take advantage only of the weak and those with untamed Stress Monkeys. Only a minority of pathogens are so deadly that they behave in a predictable way. Even so, consider 2014's Ebola outbreak. Ebola is one of the deadliest viruses known. Even the name of the virus is terrifying. Yet more than half of those who contracted the virus made a full recovery.[12] According to the germ theory, none should have survived. Why do you think everyone didn't die?

We must stop believing that there is always one cause and one cure for each disease. If the disease manifests differently in different people, then there must be a reason for that. Therefore, we must discard the monocausal approach to the treatment of disease. There are multiple causes to every disease, and one of the causes that must be considered in every case is the individual's Stress Monkey and their ability or inability to adapt to stress. So stress is bad, right?

Life without Stress

One of my favorite stories about stress is about Dr. Norman Vincent Peale. He was the author of the best-selling book *The Power of Positive Thinking*. In one instance, he was speaking to a friend who was going on and on about how many problems he had and how the stress in his life was to blame for everything that was wrong. He stated that he wished he didn't have any stress. After listening intently to this man, Dr. Peale asked his friend if he would like to meet some people who don't have any stress. To this question the gentleman gave a resounding and enthusiastic "Yes!" He stated that he would absolutely love to know where they are. Dr. Peale said there are over 150,000 of them and they are all in the Woodlawn Cemetery, in the Bronx. Dr. Peale believed that stress is a sign of life, and the more stress you have, the more alive you are.[13]

Researchers in a laboratory wanted to know what happens to living organisms when their lives are devoid of all stress. They used single-cell organisms called amoeba for this research. They placed the amoeba in an environment that was perfect for them. The temperature was perfect, and they were provided with just the right amount of nutrients—not too much and not too little. What the researchers noticed was astonishing. The cells all failed to thrive and every one of them died prematurely.[14]

So these researchers would agree with Dr. Peale. Being stress-free is equivalent to death. Let's get this straight. Stress can cause heart disease, stroke, cancer, headaches, heartburn, ulcers, and suppress our immune system, yet without stress we die. So is stress good or bad?

Stress: Good, Bad, or Neither?

Let's define the word "stress." Dr. Hans Selye defined stress as "the nonspecific reaction of the body to any kind of demand made upon it."[15] Dr. Patrick Gentempo and Dr. Christopher Kent, cofounders of the Chiropractic Leadership Alliance, told me in conversation that they define stress as "a force that causes change in your life." Notice that the definition of stress doesn't state whether it is a negative force that causes change in life. The definition also doesn't state that the changes caused by the force are always negative. The response is "nonspecific."

The fact is that your health is dependent on how well you handle stress. Actually, your success in life and in any endeavor is also entirely dependent on how well you handle stress and how much stress you can handle. Therefore, the goal should never be to eliminate stress, especially since eliminating all stress is equivalent to dying. Our goal should be to tame and empower our Stress Monkey to reduce the probability of a *negative response* to stress. Until your stress tolerance improves, do not take on any more stress than you are currently carrying.

You see, just as people handle germs differently, people also handle stress differently. Two people can be under equal stress. One person will have a heart attack as a result of that stress, and the other won't have any ill effect. Which would you rather be? One person may have a stroke, and the other will not. Which would you rather be? One may develop high blood pressure, ulcers, intestinal irritability, hormonal irregularity, headaches, and depression, while the other may not develop any of these things. Which person would you like to be? One has a wild and untamed Stress Monkey, while the other has a well-trained Stress Monkey.

Asking whether stress is good or bad is like asking whether gravity is good or bad. Or asking whether money is good or bad. What about fire? Starting a new business, obtaining higher education, expanding your family with children, chasing your dreams—all have varying degrees of stress. Are they good or bad? Stress is neither good nor bad, just as gravity, money, and fire are neither good nor bad.

Arnold Schwarzenegger attributes his life's success to the strength he developed by lifting weights. My patient Bob attributes his herniated disc to the same physical act of lifting weights in a gym. Does that mean lifting weights is good? Or is it bad?

According to a *Forbes* special report titled "America's 50 Top Givers," in 2013, William Baron Hilton donated $92 million to support his passion for ending homelessness in Los Angeles.[16] On the other hand, Osama bin Laden spent millions of dollars preparing for the September 11 attack on the United States. Does that mean money is a good thing, or is it bad?

The important concept to understand is that stress is only the force, and the Stress Monkey is responsible for responding to that force. A trained Stress Monkey can respond in a positive way by helping you become stronger and healthier, and an untrained Stress Monkey can respond in a negative way by rendering you weaker and, eventually, ill. The Stress Monkey is what determines your adaptation potential.

Each person has a different level of adaptability to stress. Imagine a paper cup placed upside down on a table. How much weight do you think it can handle? Can I place a small paperback book on it and expect it to hold? How about a large hardcover encyclopedia? How about two, three, or four large, heavy books? Eventually the cup will succumb to the weight of the books, and it will collapse. What if I use a metal cup instead of the paper cup? Will it collapse under the same amount of weight (stress), or will it be able to hold much more weight before bending? Which cup would you rather be? A cup is inanimate, but the human body can adapt. The Stress Monkey has the power to learn. The body's adaptation potential is what determines how much stress someone can handle before they succumb to illness.

Earlier I mentioned that our goal should not be to reduce stress but to reduce the probability of a negative response to stress. Stated differently, our goal should be to increase the body's adaptation potential—to tame, teach, and train our Stress Monkeys to protect us against the possibility of a negative response to stress.

As we increase the body's adaptation potential, not only do we reduce the probability of a negative response to stress; we also increase the probability of a positive response to stress.

What are some examples of a positive response to stress? One example is increased self-esteem and self-confidence. As our ability to handle stress increases, a natural response is strength of character and the confidence that comes from knowing you can handle whatever challenges may come your way.

It has been said that most multimillionaires have been bankrupt at least once before becoming wealthy. As they overcome past challenges, the stress of a financial hardship may actually create emotions of motivation, enthusiasm, and optimism instead of fear, dismay, and depression. Which set of emotions would be more conducive to success? The person with the former set of emotions has a higher adaptation potential to financial stress.

I know business owners who, under financial stress, have packed up their bags, shut down their doors, and walked away from their dreams. I also know business owners who stood their ground during tough times, found ways to innovate, and built businesses that can weather most financial storms. Who do you think had better adaptability to stress?

In the same way, a child who has contracted and overcome chicken pox now has immunity against this virus and will no longer become ill when exposed to it. Those who do not get chicken pox during childhood are at risk of a more serious illness as an adult when exposed to the same virus.

There is no question that stress can cause problems in our lives, but we are not powerless in the face of accumulated stress. We have a Stress Monkey whose sole purpose is to adapt and grow stronger under this stress. The human body and mind can adapt and grow under stress. As we adapt, we become more powerful and more resilient. We become the kind of people who can do and ultimately have the things we dream about doing and having. Taming your Stress Monkey is quite possibly the most valuable endeavor in building a life that is full of brilliant possibilities. However, before I can teach you how to tame your Stress Monkey, we need to get to know it a bit better.

CHAPTER 3

Stress and Wellness

Assumptions are made and most assumptions are wrong.

—Attributed to Albert Einstein

A common mistake people make when thinking about stress is that most people think of it only in emotional or psychological terms. However, stress can present itself in three different dimensions: physical, chemical, and psychological. With the proper training, your Stress Monkey will be quite capable of handling all three dimensions of stress.

Physical Stress

Here are some examples of stress in the physical dimension that can have a negative impact on your health:

- Prolonged sitting

- Poor posture

- Spending long hours in front of a computer

- Poor ergonomics at work

- Improper lifting

- Sleeping on an old, sagging mattress

- Contact sports

- Overtraining for athletes

- Car accidents

- Slips and falls

- Other traumatic injuries

- Being born

- Learning to walk

As mentioned earlier, your body's response to stress is much more important than the stress itself. Your Stress Monkey determines how well or how poorly your body responds and adapts to stress. For example, exercise is a stress, and, if done properly, it will lead to a positive change in the body. Resistance training with weights or bands can lead to stronger muscles and joints. Cardiovascular exercise such as running, swimming, or skiing can result in improved heart and lung function and lead to a healthier, more capable Stress Monkey.

Depending on the capacity of the Stress Monkey, you can put stress on your muscles through weight lifting, and your muscles will grow, but another person can put the same stress on their muscles and get injured. The results are entirely dependent on each person's adaptability to the specific stress. If a novice weight-lifter attempts to bench-press three hundred pounds on his first day at the gym, he will be seriously injured. But an experienced and properly trained power-lifter will have no difficulties doing the same exercise. Our focus should always be on the body's response to stress and not the stress itself.

Chemical Stress

How do chemicals affect our stress response? What we breathe in, what we ingest, and what we absorb through our skin are all stressors in the body, but they can either produce a negative result or a positive result. Sources of stress in the chemical dimension include the following:

- Air pollution
- Water pollution
- Cigarette smoke
- Secondhand smoke
- Alcohol
- Work-related hazardous materials
- Asbestos
- Antiperspirants
- Some deodorants
- Perfumes/colognes
- Drugs
- Food preservatives
- Pesticides

- Herbicides
- Cleaning agents
- Dryer sheets

And the list goes on.

Looking at this list, it might seem obvious that these items are harmful, but consider the following. Breathing oxygen typically results in a positive response by the body, but if you hyperventilate, you could pass out. Drinking pure, clean water is good for you, but drinking an excessive amount of water results in an electrolyte imbalance that can be detrimental to your health and even fatal. The same applies to certain vitamins and foods. The point again is that the body's response to stress as determined by your Stress Monkey is much more important than the source of stress.

Consider cigarette smoking. This is a stress that is detrimental to your health in any amount. The lungs are damaged by only one puff of smoke, and each subsequent puff of smoke that is inhaled will add to that damage. However, one person may smoke a pack per day for decades and never experience lung disease, whereas another person may smoke a pack a day for just ten years and develop terminal lung cancer.

Dr. Joan Schiller, professor and chief of hematology/oncology at Southwestern Medical Center, writes:

So why don't all smokers get lung cancer? Several reasons. First, one needs to accumulate a lot of these mutations before the cell becomes cancerous. Secondly, for reasons we do not completely understand, some people seem to be more susceptible to getting mutations from these cancer-causing substances than others. Finally, our bodies are remarkably good at repairing the mutations when they do happen, so in many cases they never cause the cell to become cancerous.[1]

Dr. Schiller is actually referring to your Stress Monkey here. The level of sophistication of your Stress Monkey's training determines how susceptible you are to getting mutations from these cancer-causing substances. Also, as Dr. Schiller mentions, the body has the ability to repair mutations, which is exactly why we need to get to know and tame our Stress Monkey. With proper training, your Stress Monkey can improve your resilience to, and recovery from, mutations caused by chemical stressors.

There is never just one cause for each disease. Many different factors play a role in the disease process. The person who developed cancer after smoking one pack a day for several years may also have had some vitamin deficiencies, and maybe he was also obese. Perhaps, in addition to smoking, he had a bad drinking habit, was in the middle of a divorce, and was fighting for custody of his children. These scenarios create an extreme picture, but any one of these situations would most definitely weaken the Stress Monkey and reduce the person's ability to adapt to stress. Would he have gotten lung cancer if he was otherwise in great mental and physical health? We will never know. However, we can state with great certainty that the chances of getting cancer would have been less.

Psychological Stress

That brings us to the psychological dimension of stress. Anything that can create an emotional change is considered psychological stress. The change can be positive or negative. For example, an argument with your spouse would be a stress that may cause a negative emotion. In the same relationship, intimately connecting with your spouse will result in a host of positive emotions.

Working in a job that you dislike will result in negative emotions. Working toward a goal that excites you will result in positive emotions. The stressor in this example is work, but the psychological response can vary drastically.

Dealing with financial hardship during an economic recession and worrying about job security will result in a negative response to stress. Starting a new business that is phenomenally successful, provides abundantly for your family, and produces a venue for you to express your gifts and talents will most definitely produce a positive emotional state.

Understand that every mental and emotional stress, whether positive or negative, can and should result in building up strength of character and resistance toward illness. Even if something terrible happens that results in a major emotional disturbance, the ultimate outcome can be increased mental and emotional toughness. This understanding is crucial to begin taming your Stress Monkey.

Wellness Requires You to Improve All Three Dimensions Simultaneously

To truly achieve wellness, you should train your Stress Monkey in all three dimensions of stress simultaneously. This doesn't need to be a difficult or drastic endeavor. If you begin to exercise properly but neglect the chemical and psychological dimensions, you may not achieve true wellness. If you begin to eat a balanced and nutritious diet but fail to exercise and improve the way you think, you won't attain true wellness. And if you begin to eliminate negative emotions from your psychological dimension and expect to achieve wellness without improving your dietary habits and physical rituals, you will again be disappointed. It isn't difficult to improve all three at the same time. If you make only small changes in each dimension and do them simultaneously, you will experience a noticeable improvement in your overall level of wellness.

I know many people who exercise on a regular basis, and some of them even eat an extremely well-balanced and nutritious diet, yet they still haven't reached their goals in health and fitness. That is because they haven't been addressing all three dimensions of stress and health simultaneously. Unless you take a balanced three-dimensional approach when training your Stress Monkey, you will not see any results.

Here is a good example of someone who made small changes and saw noticeable results. Robert was overweight, complained of chronic back pain, and battled depression. In the physical dimension, he changed the pillow and mattress that he slept on at night and began to exercise by going up and down the stairs in his house for ten minutes every morning. In the chemical dimension, he chose to stop taking pain killers and addressed his back problems through chiropractic care. He also increased the amount of water he drank and reduced the amount of diet soda he was drinking. In the psychological dimension, he decided that he would pray for ten minutes every day in a quiet place. He also began a collection of jokes and kept a journal in which he wrote down the funniest jokes he would hear. His friends and coworkers would constantly bring him new jokes, and he would write them down. This caused him to laugh out loud several times each day.

By making these small changes, in six months his back pain disappeared, he lost weight, and he no longer battled depression. He now plans to write two books: one will be about his transformation, and the other will be a collection of his favorite jokes. Small changes in all three dimensions of life, if done simultaneously, will have a significant impact on your overall level of wellness.

What Is Wellness?

"Wellness centers" are popping up all over the country. It's a buzzword, and marketers are having a field day with it. You can see wellness pharmacies and wellness hospitals everywhere. Massage therapists, acupuncturists, chiropractors, and nutritionists are all calling themselves wellness practitioners. How do they all define wellness? More importantly, how do you measure your level of wellness? When do you know you have achieved wellness? How will you know if your Stress Monkey is tamed?

These are very important questions, and they must be answered for us to know how to change for the better. If we don't know what wellness is, how do we know whether we're headed in the right direction?

According to the Creating Wellness Alliance, wellness is the degree to which health and vitality are experienced in every dimension of life. By definition, wellness is not a destination. It's a direction. It's like traveling east or traveling west. There is no limit to the amount of wellness you can achieve.

As you learned in Chapter 1, wellness and illness exist on a continuum, and you and your Stress Monkey are in constant motion along this continuum. You are either moving toward wellness or away from wellness and toward illness. You cannot move in both directions simultaneously, just as you cannot travel east and west simultaneously.

Every thought, action, and decision you make moves you in one of these two directions. Your daily choices are constantly pushing you back and forth on the vast spectrum of wellness and illness. All you need to do is take baby steps each day toward wellness in each of the three dimensions, and you will tame your Stress Monkey, and it will become your greatest protector against harmful stress.

Dr. Patrick Gentempo, the founder of the Creating Wellness Alliance, while speaking to a large audience at a conference I attended, asked, "Can you think of just one thing that you could be doing, that you're currently not doing, that would move you in the direction of wellness?" He shared that he has never gotten a "no" as the answer to that question. We can always think of at least one thing that we could do differently to move further in the direction of wellness. The next question Dr. Gentempo asked was "Why aren't you doing it?" That question usually seems a bit harder to answer.

I know that my typical answer would be that I don't have the time to do it. If that is your answer too, then you should sit down and reevaluate your priorities. If you want to be healthier, this is an absolute requirement. If your time is limited and every minute of your day is already accounted for, then you must choose to take time away from something and dedicate it to working on taming your Stress Monkey.

Dr. Gentempo would say that you don't need a "to-do list"; you need a "to-don't list." To practice this, make a list of things you don't need to keep doing, and free up some time. Do you need to keep reading every email in your spam box? Do you need to aimlessly surf the internet after you're done reading your email? Do you need to keep playing Candy Crush on your smartphone? Do you need to spend the next half hour on the phone with your best friend complaining about how you never have time to do anything?

As I said, to move in the direction of wellness, we must reevaluate our priorities. What do you value most in life? Is it your family? Is it your health? Is it your career? Is it your church? Do you value education? Do you value entertainment? One way to find out exactly what your core values are is to look at your bank account. How do you spend your money? After your mortgage and bills, where is the rest of your money going? If you spend your discretionary income on movies and theater, your core value could be entertainment. If you spend it on books and seminars, your core values include education.

Take a moment and determine what your true core values are. You may determine that what you truly value isn't something you actually want to value. For example, if you find out that most of your discretionary income is spent in restaurants, it would mean that you place substantial value on either dining out or the social interaction of dining out. The truth is that we give our money to the things we value most. What are your core values?

While it is important to be honest with ourselves about our true core values, it is just as important to determine our true priorities. Core values are what we give our money to, and core priorities are what we give our time and attention to. For example, someone might say that his main priority is his children. Yet he spends only half an hour per week with his children and eight hours per week playing golf. Clearly, this man is not being honest with himself about his true priorities.

To determine what your true priorities are, log how you spend your time each week. After work and sleep, what area of your life is taking up the most discretionary time? That area is your true life's priority. If you don't like the result of this exercise, then now is a good time to make a change—and be sure to dedicate some of your time to taming your Stress Monkey by improving your ability to tolerate stress in each of the three dimensions.

As a doctor, I regularly meet people who say that one of their core values is health and wellness. Yet when we discuss this further, we discover that very little of their resources, time, and money are being spent on being healthy and well. If you spend your valuable time reading this book, then health is of value and a priority to you.

All you have to do now is link it to your bigger core values. If family is your biggest core value, then consider that you can be a better parent, a better spouse, a better sibling, and a better friend if you are healthier. If your career and profession are also top core values, then link them to health and wellness by accepting the fact that you can be a better employee, a better boss, a better leader, a better producer, and a better provider for your family if you are healthier.

Also remember to consider the opposite scenario: How valuable are you to your family if you cannot take care of your own health? How valuable are you to your profession if you don't have the energy, strength, stamina, mental clarity, and longevity to work productively?

Can you enjoy life more if you are healthier? Can you enjoy your vacations more if you are healthier? Can you enjoy your hobbies and pursue your passions more if you are healthier? If your answer is yes, then make taming your Stress Monkey a priority and a core value.

Now that we agree that health and wellness are dependent on our Stress Monkey's performance, then taming the Stress Monkey should be a core value of high priority. Then the question becomes, how do we ensure that we allocate the proper amount of time, money, and energy to our Stress Monkey without neglecting our other core priorities?

Contemplating these questions reminds me of a story I read in a forwarded email. You may have seen and read this story before, and you may have heard it many times, but it is worth repeating, as its message directly affects how we view our life with regard to stress.

The story is about a college professor teaching an important lesson to his philosophy students on the first day of class. The professor placed an empty glass jar on the podium and told his students, "Consider that this jar is completely empty." He pulled out a basket of golf balls from beneath the podium and proceeded to fill the jar until he could not fit another golf ball into the jar. He asked his students if the jar was now full. The students said yes. The professor then pulled out a cup that was filled with pebbles and began pouring the pebbles into the jar. The pebbles fell in and filled the space between the golf balls. The professor then asked again, "How about now. Is the jar full?" The students again said yes. So the professor picked up a cup of sand and proceeded to pour the sand into the jar. The sand filled in the space in between the pebbles and golf balls and filled the jar to the rim. At this point, the students all agreed that now the jar was definitely full, at which time the professor brought out two cups of tea and poured them into the jar. The tea seeped into the jar and took up space between the grains of sand, the pebbles, and the golf balls, and the students laughed.

When the laughter stopped, the professor explained to the students that the glass jar represented their life. He said that we all have a finite amount of space in our jars. The golf balls represent our main priorities, such as our faith, our families, our children, our health, and so on. The pebbles are the other significant concerns of our life. They represent our second-level priorities, such as our jobs, our education, our houses, our cars, and so on. The sand represents the insignificant things in life, such as watching TV, reading the comics, doing a jigsaw puzzle, and so on. If we first fill our jar with sand, we won't have room to put the golf balls in. If we allow our lives to be filled with the insignificant things, there won't be any room for what's really important.

Then a student asked the professor what the tea represented, to which the professor answered, "No matter how busy you are, you always have time for a cup of tea with a friend."

So what are you starting with? Do you schedule prioritized time to spend with your family? Or do you fill your time with pebbles and if there's something left over, then you spend it with family? Do you schedule your exercise time in advance? Or do you say, "I'll get to it when I get to it"?

What if you scheduled your family time and workouts the same way you schedule your business meetings and your doctor's appointments? Have you ever made an appointment with yourself? It sounds a bit silly at first, but if you need thirty minutes per day to be alone in quiet so you can manage your thoughts, why not schedule it in advance and block out the time like an actual appointment? If taming your Stress Monkey is one of your "golf balls," and it should be, then you have to intentionally place it in the jar before the pebbles and the sand.

If you are still reading, then I assume you have decided to make wellness one of your golf balls, and you have made a commitment to taming your Stress Monkey. I congratulate you!

CHAPTER 4

Stress, Genes, and the Environment

It is a single cell's "awareness" of the environment, not its
genes, that sets into motion the mechanism of life.

—Bruce H. Lipton, *The Biology of Belief*

Herbert's Story

My patient Herbert was only sixty-eight years old when he died.
He died of pancreatic cancer. I absolutely loved helping Herbert
for the last ten years of his life. He was a heavyset man, somewhat
overweight with graying brown hair, and he stood about six feet
tall. He was a man of few words, but every word was always chosen
with purpose. He was an attorney but didn't practice law in the
traditional sense. He worked for a large corporation and handled

the legal aspects of the business. He was exceptionally intelligent and knowledgeable, which made him a great conversationalist. He was also extremely kind and always took the time to ask about my family. He would frequently make helpful suggestions for my next vacation or how to entertain my family better.

Approximately six years before he died, he was diagnosed with terminal pancreatic cancer. His doctor told him that he had less than a year to live and that he should get his affairs in order.

After seeing his doctor, Herbert retired from his job and decided to take a trip to Southeast Asia. He'd always wanted to go but had never made time to do so. He spent six weeks traveling and had a great time. The cancer treatment seemed to be working because Herbert felt fine, and although the cancer had spread to his spine, the tumors were growing very slowly. He was in good spirits and regularly talked about how he was "on borrowed time and enjoying it."

A few months before he passed, his oncologist started him on another round of chemotherapy. Two months later, after the chemotherapy was done, the doctor ordered a new CT scan of his chest, abdomen, and spine. The scan showed that the cancer had significantly advanced and that he had multiple new tumors in the lungs, liver, pancreas, and spine. They told Herbert that he probably had only a few days left to live.

I saw Herbert the day after he heard this news. For the first time he actually looked sick. Don't get me wrong. He had been losing a lot of weight, and he certainly didn't have the physical stature that he had ten years before, but for the first time since his cancer diagnosis six years earlier, he actually looked the part of a cancer patient. It was shocking to see how rapidly he deteriorated the minute they told him that he was near the end. He passed away a week later. I wonder if he would have lived longer if the doctors hadn't told him how sick he really was. I really miss Herbert.

The question raised by Herbert's life is this: Was Herbert's cancer a genetic condition, or was it a product of his environment? If it was purely genetic, then the doctors should have been more accurate predicting his prognosis. The doctors said he had one year left, but he lived for another six. If it was strictly environmental, then should we credit his trip to Southeast Asia with the additional five years of quality life? Neither scenario seems to explain his case, which means there must be another factor at work in this equation. Could it be that the relationship between genes and the environment is the determining factor?

The Innate Intelligence of Your Cells

We have been taught that cancer is genetic. Health-care professionals and public health authorities promote genetic screenings to see whether we are destined to contract particular diseases. They say that much of our health is restricted to the set of genes we were given from our biological parents. How does that make you feel? Do we have much control over our well-being? Will taming the Stress Monkey have any impact on our future health and longevity? Do our bodies have the ability to heal?

As long as we are alive, our bodies will continue to repair, regenerate, and regulate themselves. It's absolutely miraculous when you think about it. Our bodies are made up of cells. Cells are the basic unit of life. The human body is composed of various types of cells, and each type of cell has a different function. Some cells self-replicate and others are produced by different cells. Cell biology makes a valiant attempt to explain how these cells function.

However, the fields of biology, chemistry, and physics can provide only a limited explanation of life. Through observation, they can describe the processes of life, but they fail to explain how such processes are controlled and organized. This means there are irreducible complexities that have remained unexplainable through conventional science. As a result, many scientists have chosen to refer to the aggregate of these complexities as inborn wisdom or innate intelligence.

This is evident in the fact that technology hasn't figured out how to create life from inanimate resources. We may be able to build a mechanical model of a cell and build so much detail into it that it can actually work like a regular human cell. Perhaps it will have an outer barrier like the cell membrane that allows nutrients to come in and waste products to be excreted. Perhaps it has a power plant like the cell mitochondria that generates energy to power the cell. It can even have a program blueprint like DNA that instructs the cell how to function in different environments. The one thing we cannot do is get that cell to become self-healing and self-replicating. Current scientific technology cannot use nonliving material to build a cell that is alive. Our cells use food to rebuild, repair, and regenerate parts of themselves. The laws of physics and chemistry cannot explain this phenomenon. Yet no one can dispute the fact that living cells possess an intrinsic healing power.

Think about the origin of a human life. We know that approximately three hundred million sperm are released into the birth canal and one of those sperm cells will fertilize the egg. Studying this process, we can observe exactly what happens in each phase of fertilization, but we don't know exactly how the twenty-three chromosomes from the sperm unite with the twenty-three chromosomes from the egg to create a zygote that then develops into a ball of stem cells.

Furthermore, we know that those stem cells will differentiate into different body parts, but we don't know exactly what makes one of those stem cells develop into a brain cell and another into a bone, skin, or eye cell.

While all that is happening inside the womb, the pregnant mother begins to experience morning sickness. She is genetically preprogrammed to respond this way. Have you ever wondered why? And why is it that some women have worse symptoms than others? Is it really a sickness, or is it actually an expression of health? Throughout history, in the two instances in which morning sickness was chemically interfered with, the outcome was not favorable.[1]

During the 1950s, and possibly earlier, a drug called Thalidomide was prescribed to pregnant women for morning sickness. Birth defects resulted when Thalidomide was used to suppress the nausea of morning sickness. I believe it is dangerous to artificially suppress morning sickness, and it is equally as dangerous to put synthetic pharmaceuticals into the body during any stage of pregnancy. Both approaches can, and will, interfere with the genetic development of the baby.[2]

The American College of Obstetrics and Gynecology published the following statement in 2000: "Morning sickness has been reported to have a positive effect on pregnancy outcome and is associated with a decreased risk of miscarriage, preterm birth, low birth weight, and perinatal death."[3]

This article further states that lower nutrient intake, as caused by the nausea and vomiting of morning sickness, actually causes the placenta to develop normally. A study of malnourished women during the Dutch famine revealed that the children of women who were malnourished during all three trimesters were of lower than normal birth weight, but those women who experienced malnourishment only during their first trimester of pregnancy gave birth to babies of healthy weight.[4] In conclusion, being malnourished during the first trimester of pregnancy, whether it is caused by morning sickness or a famine, may be a good thing, as evidenced by the birth of healthy babies. Perhaps their mothers are genetically programmed to experience morning sickness to protect their babies.

So if morning sickness actually helps produce healthy babies, is it really sickness? Could this be another example of the intrinsic wisdom of life that knows exactly what to do?

And what about all the weird cravings during pregnancy? Suddenly my wife was saying that her favorite foods now made her nauseated, but foods that she previously disliked, such as fish, she craved. Could it be that the innate wisdom of her body and her genetic programming were telling her that in this stage of development, her favorite food was actually bad for the baby but fish was needed? This is yet another reason it is dangerous to interfere with morning sickness using drugs.

It is miraculous how the body knows exactly what to do when devoid of interference. This innate intelligence does not stop working after the baby is born. Consider the young child. What if he begins to feel nausea? Would you think he is sick or would you say he is healthy? The nausea could be because he put something in his mouth that should not have been ingested. His body has decided that the substance needs to come out. It will create the sensation of nausea, and the child will begin to vomit until every bit of the harmful substance has been expelled. Then, the nausea will disappear, and the child will feel fine. He is genetically programmed to respond this way.

Doesn't the same thing happen when someone drinks too much alcohol? The wisdom of the body decides that vomiting the alcohol out of the stomach is much healthier than allowing the alcohol to enter the bloodstream and cause severe alcohol poisoning, liver failure, and brain damage. How does the stomach know that more alcohol would be so harmful? How does it know that the liquid in the stomach is alcohol and not water or juice? Shouldn't we be grateful for that? Therefore, in this case vomiting is not a sign of sickness but an expression of health.

Why would a perfectly healthy child suddenly get diarrhea? As with vomiting, the body is choosing to expel something that is harmful. Certainly, the child should be monitored closely, and the child's pediatrician should be notified. However, under most circumstances, the condition should be allowed to run its course.

What does the innate wisdom of the body choose to do if the pathogen enters the body not through the mouth but through the nose and into the respiratory tract? You guessed it. The child will either cough or sneeze. If repeated coughing fails to get everything out, then his body will produce mucous to trap the "foreigners," and then he will cough up the mucous and get rid of the unwanted substances in the respiratory tract.

Why would a healthy child get a fever? Body temperature is closely monitored and carefully regulated by the innate intelligence. So when a child spikes a fever, it means his body suddenly decided it must work even harder and expend even more energy to generate more heat. Why? You're probably thinking, *Because the fever is a sign of some type of infection.* That is correct, but does this mean the child is sick or healthy?

If you were thirsty and stranded in the wilderness, would you drink water from a pond or a lake? Or would you boil the water first before you drank it? Those who are avid campers and have had wilderness training will typically say you shouldn't drink the water without first boiling it. The act of boiling the water will kill all bacteria and render the water safe to drink. In the human body, the fever is doing the same thing as boiling the water. It knows in its infinite wisdom that the harmful virus or overgrowth of bacteria cannot survive in higher temperatures. Therefore, the fever will cycle up and down until every last one of the "bugs" are dead. Once the coast is clear, the body will normalize its temperature back to, you guessed it, 98.6 degrees. Of course, all fevers must be monitored by the child's physician, but think twice before throwing in a fever reducer at the first sign of an elevated reading on the thermometer.

Your Stress Monkey is a prewritten program in your genes. Just as the body reacts to bugs and bacteria in a certain way, it is programmed to react to stress in a certain way. It is crucial to understand that a well-trained Stress Monkey will help you adapt and change in a positive way under stress, while an untamed Stress Monkey will potentially cause a breakdown of one or more of your body's natural systems.

Your Unique DNA and Your Environment

It's obvious that the body has a prewritten program that it runs on. Like a computer, the body is preprogrammed to respond in a certain way to every stimulus. This program is the human DNA. According to Dr. Bruce Lipton, the author of *The Biology of Belief*, your DNA is the blueprint that your cells use to become you.[5] Your DNA determines the color of your eyes, the color of your skin, the color of your hair, and your gender.

DNA is unique to each individual, which is why it can be used during a criminal investigation to determine whether a suspect is guilty based on DNA found at the scene of the crime. Unless you have an identical twin, no one in the world has the same DNA as you. Genes are segments of your DNA that contain information for a specific bodily function or characteristic. So, in theory, if we analyze your genetics, we should be able to predict exactly what your strengths and weaknesses are going to be, what diseases you will battle in life, and how long you are going to live. However, this statement couldn't be further from the truth.

That exact theory was the mission of the Human Genome Project: to completely map out human DNA to predict diseases in advance and devise interventions that would prevent such diseases. One of the realizations of this project, as reported in *The New York Times*, was that humans are all 99.9 percent identical.[6] I find this fascinating. If you and I are 99.9 percent identical, why do we look, feel, and act so differently, and why don't we respond to stress the same exact way? This includes people of the opposite sex. It states that even men and women are 99.9 percent genetically identical. If this is true, then where do our differences come from?

All of our body parts develop from stem cells. The human embryo is a ball of stem cells. Every one of those cells contains the exact same DNA. Then why do they differentiate into so many different body parts? If my hair cells have the same DNA as my skin cells, then why do they look and behave so differently? All of our body parts were the same at one point, but something in their environment activated a gene inside that cell that made the cell start to differentiate. This is the exact reason stem cell research is so fascinating and at the same time so controversial. Scientists have discovered that if you remove stem cells from a fetus and place them next to a living organ of another human being, those cells differentiate into that exact organ. So if you place stem cells next to a live pancreas, they become pancreatic cells, and if you put them next to a liver, they become hepatic (liver) cells. It isn't the genetics of the cell that determines what that cell becomes. It is the environment of the cell that determines which genes get expressed in that specific cell. What do you think will happen if we put stem cells next to cancer cells? How important, then, is it for us to protect our cellular environment?

Another discovery of the Human Genome Project was that there are actually twenty thousand genes in human DNA but approximately one hundred thousand different genetic characteristics. When the project was completed in 2003, the twenty thousand genes could not begin to explain the one hundred thousand different expressions of genes. The natural conclusion, according to Dr. Bruce Lipton, is that each gene can express itself in different ways, depending on environmental factors.[7]

In his book, Dr. Lipton talks about research performed with genetically identical agouti mice. One group of pregnant mice was given folic acid, vitamin B12, betaine, and choline, while the other group of genetically identical pregnant mice was fed a diet without these supplements. The mice who were given the supplements produced offspring that were brown in color, were physically lean, and had a significantly reduced incidence of obesity, diabetes, and cancer, as compared to their genetically identical counterparts who were obese, diabetic, and had a yellow coat. How could genetically identical mice be so extremely different? The supplements must have changed their cellular environment, causing their genes to be expressed differently.

Chances are that, like me, you grew up believing that your genes are the determining factor of your health. In school, we were told that we all have DNA that creates a specific code for our body and health. We believed that if our parents encountered heart disease, or cancer, or diabetes, that it was in our genetic makeup and that we were predestined to encounter those illnesses. And we were told that there was not much we could do about it. How do you feel about that?

The human body has between fifty and seventy-five trillion cells. Each cell contains the same DNA. So if someone is born with the gene for cancer, then why isn't that person born with the cancer already manifested? Why is it that it unpredictably and suddenly appears later in life? And why is it that some people with cancer in their genes don't ever get cancer?

The answer is that our genetic code for certain characteristics and tendencies is similar to having a blueprint from which a house can be built. The blueprint contains all the elements that make up the structure, but the plans have to be read by an architect to actually build the house. The architect must interpret the plans for the final product to be created. We are all genetically preprogrammed to cough, sneeze, vomit, and spike fevers, but we don't walk around all day, every day, doing those things. Only if something in our environment triggers the preprogrammed genetic response will the architect of the body read and activate those programs. Therefore, if cancer is a preprogrammed response in some of our bodies, that program still needs to be activated by an environmental trigger for the disease to manifest.

So, you may ask, why then do so many people with a family gene for cancer often develop cancer? To explore this concept, let's look at how cancer research is performed in laboratories. Mice are an excellent subject for studying genetic and hereditary causes of cancer, because, through inbreeding or genetically altering the mice, the researchers can easily replicate the type of cancer they are investigating. According to the National Cancer Institute, when these mice are exposed to a known carcinogen or a cancer-causing agent, they characteristically develop malignant tumors. The predictability of their response makes these mice ideal for studying cancer. Researchers are hoping to determine what part of their inherited genetic makeup makes them develop cancer and what prevents them from recovering from the disease.[8]

If all of them respond the same way, then it must be written in their genetic material to develop cancer, right? Absolutely and 100 percent yes. Then why do they need the cancer-causing agent? Notice that even though they have the highest genetic predisposition to contracting cancer, they still require the toxin to be introduced into their bodies to develop the cancerous tumors. The genetic program needs to be activated for the body to grow the tumors. Based on this fact, and extensive research performed by Dr. Bruce Lipton, it must be true that genes alone do not cause cancer. The gene for cancer must be turned on or activated for cancer to develop. An environmental toxin must be present, and when combined with genetic predisposition, it will result in the development of cancer. This is why many people who smoke heavily never get cancer.

So why do people with a predisposition to cancer develop cancer? Very simply put, it must be because they also get exposed to the same toxins as their relatives from whom they inherited the cancer gene. I'm not implying that their relatives poison them. I just believe the gene alone is not enough to cause the cancer. An environmental toxin must activate the gene at some point in their life.

I wonder how many of the lab mice at the National Cancer Institute would develop cancer if they weren't inbred, genetically altered, and exposed to cancer-causing toxins. For scientists to study the genetic response of these mice, some of them are injected with cancer cells, others are exposed to high doses of radiation, and others are given harmful substances such as asbestos. So they poison the mice and then study their genetic response. I fail to see how studying the genetic makeup of the mice will give us any insight into stopping the cancer epidemic. Sounds to me as though genes aren't the problem.

When it comes to how our genetic blueprint is expressed, the most important factor is our environment. People who are born with a predisposition for cancer may likely mimic environmental factors of their family, such as what they eat and where they live, as well as learned behaviors involving how they handle stress. Therefore, you should find great hope and delight in the fact that these environmental triggers are changeable and can be managed.

Dr. Lipton has written books and given hundreds of lectures about how the key factor in our health is not our genes but our environment. How we grow up, what we believe, what we eat, how we handle stress, and even how we feel about ourselves all play a role in our ultimate expression of our genetic health. We aren't born with all these elements. Instead, we develop these patterns, habits, and beliefs.

A weak foundation for health is not the result of bad genes. It is the result of making bad choices. Illness and poor health are due to toxins and deficiencies in our body. These are outside forces that can be controlled by us. This is great news, because if our genes do not determine our health, it means we can do something about our health.

Dr. Lipton further explains that a living cell cannot be in defense and growth at the same time. That means if the body is busy defending against a threat, it cannot be growing and thriving. The cells in our body will either move toward growth and health or retreat toward defense and death. In response to its environment, a cell will either express genes that promote repair and regeneration, or it will express genes that promote inflammation and illness. When we feed our body toxins, or don't supply the essential nutrients that it needs, we are literally changing our body's genetic expression. Does it seem logical to wait for illness to appear before we change our environment? The difference is between reacting to disease and preventing it on a genetic level.[9]

Our health-care system is focused more on reacting to illness than preventing it. We spend more energy, time, and money fixing problems after they occur than we do preventing them from occurring in the first place. If we focused on taming and training our Stress Monkey and increasing our adaptation potential (our ability to adapt to environmental stress), we would improve our health by leaps and bounds.

A study involving twenty-three thousand people revealed that exercising 3.5 hours a week, not smoking, eating a healthy diet, and keeping a healthy weight prevented 93 percent of diabetes, 81 percent of heart attacks, 50 percent of strokes, and 30 percent of all cancers.[10]

How important would you say it is to provide the right internal and external environment for your body? In the right environment, how much more likely is it that your Stress Monkey would work for you instead of against you in the face of stress?

Dr. Dean Ornish has been credited as being the only physician able to reverse heart disease, diabetes, and cancer without drugs or surgery. He does this by changing the patient's lifestyle and environment. "What's good for you is good for our planet," states Dr. Ornish.[11] Through his clinical studies, he has discovered that lifestyle changes worked better than drugs in not only preventing diabetes but also treating it.[12]

In his 2012 TEDx Talk in San Francisco, he explained that lifestyle and environmental changes he recommends involve only three areas: food, exercise, and love/intimacy.[13] This is completely consistent with the description of the three dimensions of stress: biochemical, physical, and psychological. It makes perfect sense that if our environment is the source of the majority of chronic diseases, then changes in this realm should make the biggest impact in our health and our ability to handle stress.

Dr. Ornish has conducted multiple landmark research studies on this subject. In 1978 he demonstrated that he could reduce arterial plaquing in ten patients within three months.[14] With specialized imaging, he demonstrated that his methods actually increased blood flow to the heart. His patients showed marked improvement within one year and continued to progress with time. In 2005 Dr. Ornish was able to reduce prostate cancer in biopsy-proven patients. In his research group, prostate-specific antigen levels dropped significantly in direct proportion to lifestyle changes.[15] He also found that his patients' lifestyle changes directly inhibited tumor growth as tested via tissue culture and as seen on magnetic resonance imaging (MRIs). In this study, Dr. Ornish was able to change gene expression in over five hundred genes in only three months. He saw an upregulation of the good genes and a downregulation of the bad ones. The bad genes were the ones that promote inflammation and oxidative stress. The downregulated genes included the ones that promote prostate cancer, breast cancer, and colon cancer.

The conclusion from Dr. Dean Ornish's work is that the same lifestyle that reverses heart disease is the same lifestyle that will prevent cancer, stroke, and diabetes. It is also the same lifestyle that will tame your Stress Monkey. In Part II, I discuss exactly how to implement a healthy lifestyle for yourself and your Stress Monkey. For now, realize and stay cognizant of the fact that the environment of your Stress Monkey will determine how it behaves. Therefore, do your best to protect yourself in all three dimensions of life: physically, biochemically, and psychologically.

Even if you are experiencing an illness right now, knowing these facts can help you tap into the healing potential that the innate power in your body wants to express. Understanding the importance of maintaining a friendly environment inside and outside the body is the key to taming your Stress Monkey and improving your quality of life.

Just as elements in our environment can activate certain genetic programs in our body, stress activates the adaptation process in our bodies. When devoid of stress, the Stress Monkey will become weak and lethargic, unable to handle the smallest amounts of stress. That's because there is nothing to adapt to.

On the other hand, under overwhelming and toxic stress, the Stress Monkey will respond by overreacting. This is because it wasn't given the opportunity to adapt properly to the stress. This results in illness or injury, like when we try to lift a weight that is too heavy or when we pull an all-nighter to meet a deadline and weaken our immune system. On the other hand, when exposed to a calculated, slow progression of increasing stress, your Stress Monkey will thrive and grow stronger. Instead of bending or breaking under the load of stress, it will learn to adapt and become more resilient.

Dr. James Chestnut, author and renowned lecturer, says, "We can only be as healthy as the environment that we live in."[16] When we have symptoms, such as a fever, vomiting, diarrhea, or something more serious, instead of searching for a way to suppress these symptoms, we should consider the environmental factors that caused them in the first place. Then we need to take the steps to create a better environment—one that does not oppose the body's innate intelligence but is conducive to healthy genetic expression.

Your future health is the result of the choices you make today. Dr. Chestnut phrases it like this: "Your health is determined by how you eat, move, and think."[17] The only reason we ever get sick is the same reason we get well, and that is based on our lifestyle and environmental choices.

In summary, Dr. Chestnut's research tells us that symptoms are signals, sent from the body to the mind to let us know that a change is necessary. The symptoms instruct us to adapt by changing our behavior and our environment. Elevation in blood pressure and cholesterol are "very intelligent and appropriate" responses to stressful situations but will result in harm if the situation remains unchanged. "Our body, since it has innate intelligence, is always adapting to provide us the best possible chance of survival in any environment, and it always does that to buy us survival time," states Dr. Chestnut. "The fight-or-flight response isn't about getting us well. It's about giving us time so we can change our environment, so we can get well."[18]

Know that your Stress Monkey comes preprogrammed with innate intelligence and is designed to learn and adapt during times of stress. The Stress Monkey's role is to help you overcome the challenges you face and, through the process, become a better, stronger, and happier person.

CHAPTER 5

The Biology of Your Stress Monkey

I am a brain, Watson. The rest of me is a mere appendix.

—Arthur Conan Doyle, *The Adventure of the Mazarin Stone*

Your Stress Monkey responds to its environment. To learn more about your Stress Monkey, let's explore what makes it react the way it does. Take a look at how this woman's Stress Monkey helped her in Spokane in 1979.

"5-Foot-3 Woman Lifts Car off Child" was a headline on the front page of the *Spokane Daily Chronicle* on December 6, 1979. "I don't know how I did it. My body hurts all over now," said forty-four-year-old Martha Weiss.[1]

How could someone that small conjure so much strength? She didn't even have time to warm up or stretch in preparation. In an instant she became superwoman. The article said that she weighed only 118 pounds. Yet she was able to do something that during normal circumstances she would not be able to do. How did she do it? Her Stress Monkey helped her.

In this chapter, I discuss the interface between the outside environment and DNA, which is made up of genes. If our DNA is isolated in the nucleus at the center of each of our cells, how does it know what's going on outside the human body?

Take a look at how the body works. If you wanted to move your index finger, how would you do it? "I would just do it" is probably your response. Well, how come the other fingers in your hand don't move? Why doesn't the index finger in the other hand move? What gives you control over your hands and fingers?

I just asked my five-year-old son that very question with multiple-choice answers. The choices were "the heart," "the belly," "the head," and "the finger moves all by itself." He answered, "It's my brain, in my head."

Has your hand ever fallen asleep? For example, at night, have you woken up to find that one of your hands is completely numb? Do you still have full control of your fingers at that moment? If you are a master piano player, would you be able to play the piano at that moment? What do you think caused this temporary loss of function? Is it similar to someone who is paralyzed and cannot use or control their limbs? If you are thinking about spinal cord trauma, you're on the right track.

Your Brain and Your Nervous System

Nerves relay information from the brain to the various parts of the body. Your brain tells your finger to move, and that information travels along the path of a nerve all the way from the brain to your finger, and then, and only then, the finger moves. If that nerve is no longer connected to your finger, the finger will not move. The brain may keep telling your finger to move, but if the nerve signal doesn't reach the muscles that move your finger, the finger will never move.

Then how does the brain know that it has accomplished its mission of moving the index finger? Is it because your eyes saw your finger move? Try moving your index finger again, but this time, close your eyes. You should have noticed that you felt the finger move. You didn't need to see it move to know that it moved. The brain received feedback from the targeted body part, in this case the index finger, informing the brain that the task was accomplished. The same applies to every joint in your body. You don't have to look down at your knees to know if they are bent or straight. Taking this a step further, you don't need to look at yourself in the mirror to know if you're wearing long pants, shorts, or a skirt. You know if it's warm or cold, dark or light, or wet or dry outside, and all of this information travels through neural pathways from the outside environment to the brain. So not only is the brain a command center that controls your actions; it is also a receiving station that monitors and surveys the outside environment.

The brain is what activates the programs stored in your genes. Information is relayed to the brain from the outside environment. The brain then decides which programs need to run and which genes need to be activated. Then the information is sent out to the specific body parts, and those body parts are instructed by the brain how to act in response to the environment.

Let's learn a bit more about the brain. Is the brain the most important and vital part of your body? Or is the heart the most vital part? The heart functions to circulate oxygen-rich blood throughout the body. If we used a machine to pump the blood through the blood vessels, we would be able to keep the body alive without a heart. What about the lungs? Again, we can use a machine to force air in and out of the lungs or artificially oxygenate the blood to keep the body alive.

Advancements in surgical procedures actually enable us to have heart and lung transplants. That means a surgeon can replace someone's heart or lungs with those of an organ donor and successfully save a life. It's incredible what a surgeon can do. The same can be done with kidneys and the liver.

Is there an organ in the body that can never be transplanted? Is there an organ in the body that is more vital to life than all other organs? Is there an organ in the body that sustains life and controls all other organs in the body? Yes, you guessed correctly; it's the brain.

When I was studying in school, one of my classes was gross anatomy. For four continuous trimesters, during the first two years of the program, I dissected the entire human body for several hours each week. I had to identify every organ, muscle, bone, tissue, and gland. I had to trace every blood vessel, artery, and vein back to the heart, and I had to trace every nerve back to the spine. I discovered that there is a nerve that goes to every tissue, gland, and organ in the human body, and all those nerves are connected to the brain. The brain is connected to all other body parts to control all bodily functions.

Earlier I define health as proper function and not just the absence of symptoms and disease. Since the brain controls all the functions of the body, then the brain must be directly responsible for how healthy we are. If, for example, I disconnect the brain from my index finger, will I still be able to move that finger? Is that just a theory, or is that an absolute fact? If I damage the nerves to my right arm, will I still have full use of my right arm? Of course not. Not only will I lose the ability to move my arm; I will also lose the ability to sense and feel with my fingers.

Your limbs are in constant and continuous contact with your brain. There are nerve signals that repeatedly travel from your extremities to your brain, constantly reminding your brain of the status of the joints. These are called sensory nerves. Sight, sound, touch, taste, smell, and joint position are all examples of information that regularly travels from the outside world to the brain through these nerves. If the nerve signals from one of the legs stops reaching the brain, we say that the leg has "fallen asleep." This sensation can be replicated by sitting on one end of the couch with your legs dangling over the arm rest for an excessively extended period of time (don't try this!). After a few minutes, one or both of the legs will fall asleep. At that point, the leg is numb, and if you try to walk, you won't be able to feel the floor. It will feel as if you're walking on stilts. This is all because the compression of the nerves from your leg has blocked all communication between your leg and your brain. This information helps you balance yourself when walking, and if it is interrupted, you will easily lose your balance and fall.

The minute your brain realizes that it hasn't heard anything from one of your legs, it starts to search for the leg. Since no information is reaching the brain from the leg, the brain will make that leg hypersensitive, and the leg will become overly sensitive to any stimulation. At that moment, light touch actually feels like pins and needles. Movement of the leg also causes tingling. In fact, the leg may be so sensitive that it becomes uncomfortable to move the leg. However, if you shake the leg and stimulate the nerves, the sensitivity will normalize, and your leg will begin to feel normal again. Shaking the leg sends a burst of neurological input to the brain, letting it know that the leg is intact and communication has been reestablished. At that moment the hypersensitivity and pins-and-needles will start to go away, your balance will be restored, and you will have complete control of your leg again.

Your Brain and Your Circulatory System

It is easy to see the relationship between nerves and voluntary movement, but that's not the only thing your brain controls through nerves. Did you know that your brain controls the flow of blood throughout your body? Think about a moment when you were seriously embarrassed. Like having toilet paper stuck to your shoe, or waving at someone you thought you knew but who turned out to be a stranger. The minute you get embarrassed, your face will flush, and if your skin isn't too tan, you will "turn red."

What causes the face to flush or turn red? The answer is increased blood flow. When your mind perceives something as embarrassing, it sends a signal through a specific set of nerves to the skin of the face. The brain tells the small blood vessels (capillaries) of the face to dilate and increase blood flow to the face, in turn causing the face to appear flushed. You see, the face itself doesn't get embarrassed. Information travels to the brain through your sensory nerves, such as sight and sound, and the brain interprets that information as embarrassing. Then, it responds by sending signals to the capillaries of your face.

Let's look at another example of how the brain controls blood vessels and circulation. Think about a time when you were scared for your life—like a near-miss car accident that could've been disastrous, or suddenly realizing that you left your purse or briefcase in the taxi that is driving away. Chances are, if you were really scared, your face turned pale white, reminiscent of the expression "You look like you've just seen a ghost." The mechanism is the same. Your eyes sent the sensory information to your brain, and your brain quickly interpreted the situation as dangerous. At that moment, it sent signals to several body parts to prepare for the potential disaster. By constricting certain blood vessels and dilating others, it took blood from your skin and sent it to your muscles to prepare them for fast action, such as smashing the brake pedal or sprinting to catch a bus. When the blood leaves your face, you turn pale. The signals from the brain also tell the pupils of your eyes to dilate so that you can let in more light and see your surroundings differently. This process is called the sympathetic response to stress, and a well-trained Stress Monkey will be able to manage all this for you. It is commonly known as the fight-or-flight response. This physiological response is what enabled our five-foot-three Martha Weiss to be able to lift a car off the child.

Even the flow of blood is under the direct control of the brain and nervous system. While the brain's control of muscles and joints is voluntary, the brain's control of blood flow is involuntary. In other words, you can easily decide when and how to move your index finger, but more than likely you cannot increase the flow of blood toward your left kidney. Can you make your heart stop beating right now? Can you make it stop beating even for just a minute? Yet your heart actually knows when it should beat faster and when it should slow down. How does it know these things? The answer is that your heart and many of your other organs and glands are under the control of the autonomic nervous system. That refers to the areas of the brain that automatically control essential functions of the body that keep you alive. The good news is you will never accidentally forget to make your heart beat. It is automatically controlled by your brain without the requirement of conscious thought. In fact, when you think of the autonomic nervous system, just think of the word "automatic." Your Stress Monkey is the autonomic nervous system. If left untrained, there will be chaos and disharmony among the organs, glands, and blood vessels, leading to an unhealthy response to stress.

Your Autonomic Nervous System

Earlier in this chapter, I discuss the sympathetic response to stress, which is more commonly referred to as the fight-or-flight response. It is the response that allowed the woman in Spokane to lift a car when needed. This is one of those automatic functions under the influence of your Stress Monkey. The autonomic nervous system serves two purposes in the body. One is called the sympathetic response, and the other is called the parasympathetic response. This system can be likened to a car that has a gas pedal and a brake pedal. The sympathetic nervous system is like the gas pedal and is used to speed up certain functions, such as heart rate and metabolism. The parasympathetic system, more commonly referred to as the rest-and-digest response, is used to slow down those same functions. Since you don't have direct control over these two pathways, it is critical to train your Stress Monkey to help you manage these processes in a healthy way.

When the sympathetic nervous system is activated—such as when a car is on top of a child—the adrenal glands will release adrenaline, the heart will beat faster, and breathing intensifies. The pupils of the eyes dilate to let in more light. This is when blood is drawn away from the skin and certain internal organs, such as the stomach and the intestines. Most of the blood is directed by the nervous system to supply the muscles with oxygen and nutrients. In this instance, digestion completely stops, and the body is prepared to take actions related to fight-or-flight. When I was on the track team in high school, I regularly saw our elite athletes throw up right before the big race. This happened because they were in fight-or-flight mode and digestion had seized, so their body had to get rid of their stomach contents.

The opposite of the sympathetic nervous system is the parasympathetic nervous system. The parasympathetic system is activated when there is no perceived danger. Imagine that you just ate a large and delicious meal that you thoroughly enjoyed. Now you are lounging on the couch, your legs are outstretched, and your feet are on the coffee table. You are so relaxed that you are about to doze off into a deep peaceful sleep. This is the parasympathetic response, and that is why it is commonly referred to as the rest-and-digest or wine-and-dine response. In this instance, most of the blood flow is directed toward the intestines and the stomach to promote digestion. The more relaxed you are, the better your body can digest the food and use the nutrients to supply the rest of your body. All healing, repair, and regeneration of tissues, organs, and glands occur under the control of the parasympathetic nervous system. This is why I personally like to call it the rest-and-repair division of the nervous system.

All of this occurs automatically outside of your voluntary control. However, you do have a degree of influence on the overall autonomic responses of your body. For example, you can activate your parasympathetic system by eating a large meal, doing a breathing exercise, meditating, or sleeping. You can also activate your sympathetic response by worrying, watching a horror movie, gambling, or taking a polar plunge in arctic waters. When we worry, the body responds in the same way as when something bad actually happens. The emotions of worry, fear, anger, and anxiety can activate the sympathetic response, whereas emotions of love, joy, gratitude, and hope will most likely stimulate a parasympathetic response. This is how Dr. Ornish was able to reverse cancer, heart disease, and diabetes—by stimulating and activating the rest-and-repair system while maintaining a clean environment inside and around the body. Since all healing, repair, and regeneration occur in the parasympathetic state, which emotions would you rather experience more often?

Balancing the Sympathetic and Parasympathetic Nervous Systems

Chapter 4 talks about Dr. Lipton's work and his conclusion that a cell cannot be in growth and defense at the same time. Similarly, the body cannot be in a fully sympathetic and fully parasympathetic state at the same time. This would be like pressing the gas pedal and the brake pedal of a car at the same time. The car wouldn't know what to do. The engine would rev, the car would jerk, but it wouldn't actually go anywhere. In the same way, you cannot sleep if you are in sympathetic overdrive. That would be like relaxing into a deep comfortable sleep while being chased by a pack of hungry wolves. The instant the wolves appear, you will enter a state of heightened awareness. Your Stress Monkey will flip the on switch to your fight-or-flight system. You will be more alert than if you had just consumed a hundred cups of coffee (don't try this!).

Both the sympathetic and parasympathetic systems are necessary for survival, and there needs to be balance between the two systems. An imbalance between the two can be very detrimental to your health. Unfortunately, in today's fast-paced world, many people are living their life in sympathetic dominance. That means their untrained Stress Monkey has their body operating in a constant state of fight-or-flight. Over the past twenty-four hours, if you worried about money or paying your bills, you activated the sympathetic system. If you had an argument with a family member or yelled at your kids, you activated the sympathetic nervous system. If you got stuck in traffic, were late for work, got yelled at by your boss, missed a deadline, or received bad news, you are most likely in sympathetic overdrive. Simply watching the news can send you into sympathetic overdrive, especially if there's been yet another school shooting or viral outbreak.

Normally it wouldn't be a problem to have a fight-or-flight response to an event, especially if it helps you lift a car off a child, as long as your Stress Monkey has time to balance itself with time spent in a parasympathetic state of rest-and-repair. Unfortunately, many of us today don't even take time to sit down and enjoy a nice lunch. Instead, we eat on the go, in our car, or at our desk while working on the computer. How can our Stress Monkey attempt to rest and digest if we are always in a state of heightened awareness? If the body has no time to heal, repair, and regenerate in the parasympathetic state, it will begin to break down and decay. The body was not designed to remain in sympathetic overdrive long term. Taming your Stress Monkey will create the fail-safe system that will snap you out of a sustained period of fight-or-flight mode.

Do not mistakenly link the state of sympathetic overdrive with feeling emotional stress. Even if you are not emotionally experiencing a lot of stress, the act of not resting or relaxing can be severely detrimental to your health. This concept makes me think of technology greats such as Steve Jobs and Elon Musk, among many others. Throughout the years of their stellar careers, they regularly put in long hours of work without much rest. In an interview with *The New York Times*, Elon Musk stated that he frequently works 120 hours per week.[2] Neither Jobs nor Musk ever reported feeling any stress from their work, and, in fact, they claimed to enjoy work. Meanwhile, they did not and do not allow time for their bodies to rest and repair.

Even when you do not feel stress, you may be in a state of sympathetic overdrive—your Stress Monkey may be running amok without your knowledge. Today, there are many young professionals striving for success in their field, and they're filling their bodies with unhealthy stimulants and energy drinks so that they can stay alert and productive through long workdays. This behavior keeps their bodies in sympathetic overdrive. Their bodies will not last, because they are not allowing enough time for the parasympathetic nervous system to activate the processes of healing, repair, and regeneration.

The exact opposite of this is the French paradox. In France, the incidence of heart disease is very low when compared to other Western nations. However, their intake of saturated fats and cholesterol-rich foods is very high.[3]

Hence the paradox: If their diet is so bad, then why don't they have more heart attacks? I believe the answer lies in the French culture and their attitude toward food and eating. As an American vacationing in France, I couldn't help but notice how much longer the French spend at the dining table during mealtime. Our dinners would last at least two hours.

In the United States, it is common to tell your restaurant server that you are in a hurry and ask them to bring your check when the food comes out. Such behavior in France would be misconstrued as disrespect for the food, the chef, and the restaurant. So, as it is their culture, the French typically sit down and relax when they eat, and they take their time, eating slowly and savoring every bite. Which side of the nervous system do you think this behavior will activate? If you said wine-and-dine or rest-and-digest, you are correct. This is the embodiment of the parasympathetic nervous system.

Who do you think will process their food in a healthier fashion: The American couple who is rushing through their meal because they're worried about missing the show or the start of the play? Or the French couple who is calmly enjoying their meal and in no rush to leave the restaurant?

Food is intended to stimulate the parasympathetic response, which in turn promotes proper digestion, strengthens the immune system, slows the heart rate, decreases blood pressure, and creates an environment in your body that is ideal for rest, repair, and regeneration. When we eat on the go, rushed and nervous, we stay in sympathetic overdrive and never really process our food properly. How we eat is just as important as, and perhaps even more important than, what we eat. The person who eats super healthy foods but rushes through his or her meal is more likely to have a heart attack than the person who may not eat as many healthy foods but maintains a peaceful state of mind while eating.

This is why a major step in taming your Stress Monkey is forcing yourself to spend time in rest-and-repair. You do this by eating slowly and savoring each bite of your food. You also do this by not watching the news before bedtime. You do this by limiting stimulants, such as sodas and energy drinks, and by reading and applying the steps in this book.

Lauren's Story

My patient Lauren is an eighth-grade schoolteacher for the public school system. Her chief complaint was that once or twice a week, she woke up with a stiff neck and had trouble turning her head. Anti-inflammatories and pain medications were helpful, but the stiffness always returned a few days later. As we spoke about her condition, I realized that she had a long list of symptoms she had assumed were unrelated to her stiff neck. Some of the symptoms she complained about included the following:

- Cold hands and feet
- High blood pressure
- High cholesterol
- Indigestion
- Acid reflux
- Constipation

- Insomnia
- Frequent head colds
- Frequent sinus infections
- Dry skin
- Inability to lose ever-increasing belly fat

Lauren was treated by a number of specialists: a cardiologist who prescribed medication for high blood pressure and high cholesterol, a gastroenterologist who suggested over-the-counter antacids and stool softeners, and a primary care physician who prescribed a low-dose sedative for insomnia and recommended that she continue to take ibuprofen for her recurrent neck pain.

She was also advised that she was prediabetic and that if she didn't lose weight, she would wind up with diabetes. However, she considered herself healthy, because she believed the medications were "making" her healthy.

So I asked her, "How's your Stress Monkey?" Just kidding! That's not exactly what I asked her. I asked how she handled stress in her life.

As a junior high school teacher, she dealt with preteens, young teenagers, and their crazy hormones. The parents of her students regularly blamed her for their child's lack of effort and poor grades. She was also experiencing an enormous amount of pressure from the school administration that constantly changed the curriculum. And she had to spend her spare time grading papers and preparing lesson plans, for which she felt underpaid and unappreciated.

From the details of her life, it is pretty obvious that Lauren was stuck in sympathetic overdrive. Her body was in a constant state of fight-or-flight. Although her team of physicians had separated her different symptoms into distinct categories, I felt certain that they were all related.

Let's break it down. The first sign of sympathetic activation is an increased heart rate, which causes high blood pressure. When the state of fight-or-flight persists or recurs too frequently, cortisol levels will increase. Cortisol is commonly known as the stress hormone. It is produced by the adrenal glands—the same glands that produce adrenaline during stressful times. While adrenaline may help you lift a car, cortisol helps the body use sugar and fat as energy. It mobilizes triglycerides and cholesterol in the blood. Triglycerides and cholesterol are precursors to other very important hormones, such as estrogen and testosterone. This is why someone who has elevated blood pressure as a result of chronic sympathetic overdrive will also have elevated serum cholesterol levels. Artificially lowering cholesterol using drugs without addressing the cause or meeting the hormonal needs of the body is not a permanent solution to the problem.

Why were Lauren's hands cold all the time, even during the summer? Recall that when faced with a dangerous situation that elicits a fight-or-flight response, the body will constrict blood vessels in the skin and the extremities to direct that blood to the muscles in preparation for emergency action. When Lauren is in chronic sympathetic overdrive, her hands and feet will naturally have poor circulation, which renders them constantly cold with dry skin.

During the fight-or-flight response, the body stops all digestive activities to direct the blood and other resources to the muscles. When being chased by the proverbial saber-toothed tiger, your brain isn't worried about whether you're digesting your food. No wonder Lauren had indigestion, heartburn, and constipation. Her body was always preparing for a fight and wasn't taking enough time to focus on resting and digesting.

This is the same reason Lauren would get frequent head colds and sinus infections. Too often, her body was taking resources away from the immune system and directing those resources to her large muscles to give them what they needed to escape the proverbial saber-toothed tiger or lift the car off the child. Chronic sympathetic overdrive significantly weakens the immune system.

How is all this related to her prediabetic status? As mentioned earlier, cortisol increases blood sugar levels, because sugar is the fuel that sustains muscle activity. In the short term this is a healthy and useful response to stress. However, elevated blood sugar levels sustained over a long period of time will eventually result in diabetes. Naturally, cortisol tends to increase appetite and odd cravings to maintain such high energy states of blood sugar and cholesterol. As a result, people in this type of chronic sympathetic overdrive tend to gain excessive belly fat, which is nearly impossible to lose if the patient stays in the state of fight-or-flight.

It may sound as though I'm blaming everything on the hormone cortisol. That's not the case. Cortisol is very beneficial to the body, and a well-trained Stress Monkey knows exactly how to vary cortisol levels in a cyclical manner throughout the twenty-four-hour circadian cycle. However, when excessive amounts of the hormone are released without giving the body a chance to recover, it will result in the following:

- Blood sugar imbalance
- Decreased bone density and osteoporosis
- Sleep disruption
- Decreased muscle mass
- Elevated blood pressure
- Lowered immune function
- Increased abdominal fat
- Increased inflammation in the body

It is that last item on this list that explains the recurring neck pain and stiffness Lauren was experiencing. Recall that she said the over-the-counter anti-inflammatories helped her feel better, but the pain kept coming back. Anti-inflammatories help only if the cause of the problem is inflammation.

An individual who is under constant negative emotional stress and has trouble sleeping at night probably has a tendency to be very tense in her neck and shoulders. The whole thing is the perfect storm and a recipe for disaster. Her problem is not a musculoskeletal issue. It is not a gastrointestinal issue. It certainly is not a cardiovascular issue. This is a nervous system issue, and the only solution is for Lauren to tame her Stress Monkey. Otherwise, this will not end well.

Lauren's story had a happy ending. I was able to restore balance between her sympathetic and parasympathetic nervous systems. Once this balance was reestablished, her symptoms began to disappear. She gradually went off all medication and even began to lose weight. All of this was accomplished by implementing the steps and protocols in this book.

CHAPTER 6

Your Brain and Your Stress Monkey

The only person you are destined to become
is the person you decide to be.

—Nike advertisement, 1991

We have spent a lot of time discussing sympathetic overdrive and less time discussing parasympathetic dominance. The reason is that in today's culture parasympathetic overdrive is not too prevalent. However, to be fair, let's spend just a few minutes on that right now. This can occur if your Stress Monkey is overly exhausted or extremely lazy.

Similar to sympathetic dominance, parasympathetic overdrive can result in negative symptoms. These may include increased salivation, abnormally low blood pressure, increased mucous production, bronchial constriction that can cause wheezing in the lungs, being overly emotional, and increased/frequent urination. This is exactly why autonomic balance is so important to our health.

Your Brain and Your Spinal Column

As we have seen, the brain controls all functions of the body. The spinal cord is the information highway that allows for the transmission of information from the brain to the body parts and from the environment back to the brain. This explains why damage to the spinal cord can be so detrimental to the body.

On May 27, 1995, Christopher Reeve was thrown from a horse during an equestrian competition in Virginia. The fall caused irreparable damage to his spinal cord. As a result, he required a wheelchair, a pacemaker, a breathing apparatus, and assistance with bowel and bladder functions for the rest of his life. Before his injury Mr. Reeve was an actor, famous for his role as the iconic Superman. Why is it that after his injury, Superman could no longer move his arms and legs and lost other bodily functions, including his ability to breathe? Did he damage his lungs in the fall? No. Did he injure his arms and legs? No.

His injury was to the neck. If the brain controls all those functions, and the injury occurred below the brain, in the spinal cord, then why did he lose so many functions? The answer is that the vital information from the brain was no longer able to travel down the spinal cord into his organs, his arms, and his legs. It is obvious that the spinal cord is just as important as the brain when it comes to the health and function of the body. Neither one can sustain life without the other.

Here's where it all becomes very interesting. Visualize for an instant that you are in front of the New York Philharmonic, witnessing a

masterful display of musical talent from the musicians who beautifully accompany each other in tone, pitch, rhythm, and volume. The
result is breathtaking. So what's with the guy wearing the long tail
tuxedo, standing up front, waving the stick at the musicians? He's not
making any musical sounds, right? Why is he there?

He's the conductor! The orchestra can't perform without him.
What would happen if one of the musicians had an obstructed view
and couldn't see the conductor? He or she might not be able to
keep up with the rest of the orchestra, and this musician might
even ruin the sound of the entire orchestra. In this scenario, did
this poor musician suddenly lose her musical talent? Or did this
happen because of the obstruction blocking her view of the conductor? Clearly it was the latter. I share this scenario to demonstrate
how the obstruction that prevented the musician from performing
well mirrors the spinal cord injury (obstruction) that Christopher
Reeve suffered.

Your brain is always doing what the conductor of the orchestra
is doing. It is sending information out to the various tissues of the
body to ensure that your body continues to play its proverbial music.
If there was ever an obstruction in the system of nerves, such as a
spinal cord injury, the brain (conductor) would not be able to get the
message out to a certain organ (musician).

The consequence of this would be disastrous. What if this obstruction affected communication between the brain and the heart?
Would the heart continue to function the way the brain wanted it
to? In a case like this, there is nothing wrong with the heart itself,
and there's certainly nothing wrong with the brain, but there is miscommunication between the brain and the heart, causing the heart
to have trouble keeping up with the rest of the organs (musicians). In
this instance, intervention is necessary. The question is, what type of
intervention should be used? Should it be in the form of chemicals

that bypass the nervous system and artificially control the heart? Or should it be focused on restoring communication between the brain and the heart?

Your Brain and Your Digestive Process

Did you know that twenty separate organs need to work together for you to digest your food? The minute your nose smells food, your digestive system goes to work. Even something as simple as seeing a picture of appetizing food activates your digestive tract. You begin to salivate. Your stomach begins to produce acid. Your pancreas will begin to release the enzymes needed to digest the particular food you just smelled. For example, if what you smelled is a high-protein food, the pancreas will produce protease, an enzyme that breaks down proteins and peptides. Lipase gets released by the pancreas if the food is high in fats. If the food you smelled is a high-carbohydrate meal, your pancreas will more likely produce amylase, an enzyme that converts starch and glycogen into simple sugars. Then the pancreas will release the hormone insulin to prepare for the potential increase in blood sugar. You get the point. This process goes on and on until all food is digested and absorbed into the various tissues of the body.

The liver and the gallbladder don't have any sensory perception devices. This means the gallbladder doesn't ask the stomach what's coming its way. It doesn't have its own eyes to see what's in the stomach, and it doesn't have its own nose to smell the food in the stomach. The gallbladder waits until it receives instructions from the brain. If the fat content of the food is high, the brain will tell the gallbladder to squeeze and flush the concentrated bile into the beginning section of the small intestine to help in fat breakdown. This happens with every single organ involved in digestion. Each organ must be instructed by the brain, and the brain carefully monitors and coordinates the efforts of all the organs to produce the desired outcome.

Now, you may think that the desired outcome of digestion is to turn food into energy for the body. The reality is that proper digestion not only replenishes the energy sources of your body but also provides nutrients used for building, repair, and regeneration of all body parts. That means your body, under the control of your brain, can take a salad and turn it into liver cells to keep your liver alive.

Did you know that your cells are constantly being replaced? For example, your skin cells live only about thirty days before they need to be replaced. The lining of your stomach gets replaced every five days, and your taste buds get replaced about every ten days.

Therefore, digestion is not just about turning food into energy. Under the control of your nervous system, your digestive system can change the molecular structure of the foods you eat and turn them into actual body parts. How incredible! This is why it is so important to make sure the connection and communication between the brain and the rest of your body is perfectly maintained, without any interference.

PART II

TEN STEPS TO TURN STRESS INTO STRENGTH AND MOVE TOWARD HEALTH AND WELLNESS

CHAPTER 7

Step One: Get Adjusted

It is more important to know what sort of person has a
disease than to know what sort of disease a person has.

—Anonymous, "Passing of Pathognomonic Symptoms"[1]

Based on anatomical, neurological, and physiological evidence, the connection between the brain and the body is a critical factor in determining the overall health of the body. Therefore, maintaining clear channels of communication between the brain and the various organs can significantly reduce the chance of illness and increase your adaptability to stress (tame your Stress Monkey). Open communication between the brain and the digestive tract results in better digestion and ultimately better health through repair and regeneration. Constant communication between the brain and the cardiovascular system results in better heart function and reduced risk of heart disease. Proper communication between the brain and the musculoskeletal system results in better coordination and a reduced chance of musculoskeletal injury. The nervous system also controls the immune system, and a nervous system devoid of interference will result in better resistance to opportunistic pathogens and infections. There isn't a single realm of human health that will not positively benefit from an optimized nervous system.

Let me tell you an inspiring story that illustrates the power of these connections.

Dr. Watson's Story

Dr. Kevin Watson and his wife, Dr. Marcia Watson, own and operate a successful chiropractic practice in Edmonton, Alberta, Canada. The following passage recounts the real-life story of Kevin Watson in his own words.

> When I was four years old, medical specialists told my parents that I was permanently brain damaged. I've been arguing with these so-called specialists ever since.
>
> Shortly after being born, I started throwing febrile seizures. My body temperature would rise, and when it spiked, I would go into convulsions. At first the doctors thought that the seizures were caused by an infection, so they prescribed high doses of antibiotics. The antibiotics didn't help, but my parents reluctantly followed the doctors' advice, changing and filling one prescription after another. My mother disliked the idea of drugging her infant son but hated witnessing the seizures even more. She begged the doctors to try something other than antibiotics. The doctors reasoned that since my seizures always followed a fever, all my mother had to do was

keep my body temperature down with high doses of Tylenol and ice baths.

My mother was so tired of feeding me drugs that she opted for the ice baths. When my temperature started to rise, she would run to the freezer and grab all the ice and empty it in the bathtub, run cold water, and hold me in the tub of freezing water until the temperature subsided. She said it was awful. I would be kicking and screaming, but she would pin me down and hold me in the tub for as long as it took. At first, this technique would shock my central nervous system enough to impede the convulsions, but the frequency of the fevers increased over time. My poor mother. Sometimes my fever would spike before the water in her ice trays refroze. She was so determined that the ice baths were going to cure the seizures that she would grab me under her arms and run through the neighborhood screaming at the top of her voice that she needed ice. The neighbors thought she was nuts, but one lady would always open her door, empty all of her ice in her bathtub, and help my mother pin me down until the fever subsided.

As I got older, the seizures worsened, and they were having a harder and harder time holding me down in the ice baths. There was only so much kicking and screaming that they could take. That is when they demanded to see some more specialists. The first specialist said that I must have meningitis and the only way to test for that was by doing a spinal tap. They informed my father that he would have to hold me in the fetal position while they withdrew some cerebrospinal fluid from my spine.

My dad is a tough-looking cowboy. At the time he was also the coach of the high school football team, so the doctors thought he would be able to hold me down just fine. The thing with most tough-looking guys is that they are soft as hell in the inside. My mother said that as soon as they brought the needle out to perform the spinal tap, the kicking and screaming began. It turns out Dad has a terrible fear of needles, and he was crying his heart out as he held me in the fetal position while the specialist jammed a six-inch needle into my spine.

The spinal tap came back negative for meningitis, but the specialists decided to give me the meningococcal antibiotic anyway. My father was infuriated. Why did they have to perform a spinal tap, if they were just going to prescribe the same drugs, regardless of the lab results? What kind of risks were they taking by sticking a needle into the spine of a child? What the hell was wrong with these so-called specialists?

The antibiotic didn't help, and six months later we were at a new specialist's office. These doctors convinced my parents to perform an electroencephalogram to measure brain-wave activity. They had instructed my parents to shave all the hair off my head and to be prepared to help out.

This was the mid-1970s, and medical technology wasn't near what it is today. The nurses rolled in a strange-looking machine with a dozen or so wires hanging from it and asked my father to help them hold me down. He wasn't sure what to expect and nearly lost his mind when they started plunging the bare wire leads deep into my skull. I was four years old, and, although I don't have much recollection of any of my childhood, I remember that test. It hurt like hell! I was kicking and screaming and being held down by my mother, while across the room, my dad was kicking and screaming and being held down by the nurses.

The electroencephalogram test results came back positive, in a very negative way. The specialists sat my parents down and told them I had epilepsy and permanent brain damage. They explained that parts of my brain were not functioning and that I would never be able to read or write, play sports, or attend a "normal" school. They said the epilepsy could be treated with more drugs but that a seizure could occur at any time. Because of this, they recommended that I wear a helmet anytime I was outside.

My parents left this appointment completely devastated. They drove to the pharmacy and filled the prescriptions of phenobarbital, Dilantin, and more antibiotics. Then they drove to a sports store and got me fitted for a stupid white helmet. While I don't remember much about my childhood, I do remember that stupid white helmet. I hated that damn thing!

I was five years old, and nobody wore helmets back then. I would go outside to play road hockey with my older brother and the neighborhood kids, and I was the only one wearing a helmet. Even the goalie would be in a net with a couple of phone books taped to his shins, but no helmet. The taunts of "Hey, helmet-head" and "What's the matter, Crash Baby" were unyielding. I got so frustrated that I would walk over to the side of the street and pick up all the small rocks and put them in my pockets. When the kids would tease me, I would throw the rocks at them, and a full-out rock fight would ensue!

My poor mother was losing her mind! She couldn't let me go outside to play without my helmet, because she was terrified that I would have a seizure and crack my head open. But if I went outside with the helmet on, I would end up throwing rocks at the neighborhood kids and could possibly crack their heads open. She had now been coping with over five years of seizures, drugs, ice baths, spinal taps, electroencephalograms, and now rock fights. She was stressed out and needed help! This is when one of the neighborhood ladies suggested she go see her chiropractor, Dr. Clark Lundgren.

Dr. Lundgren practiced in a town two hours away, so my mom strapped that stupid white helmet to my head, packed my bag of prescription drugs, and took me along for the ride. She went in to get her adjustment and came out feeling great. As she was packing me up to leave, Dr. Lundgren came out and asked, "Irene, does your son throw seizures?" She answered, "Yes, how did you know that?"

He said that he noticed my ear was much lower on one side than the other and that one eye was drooping. He explained that if the skull doesn't sit properly on top of the spine, the central nervous system can be stressed and seizures will manifest. He then asked my mother about my birth. She said the birth had been awful and that the doctors had rushed the delivery using a great deal of force with forceps. She told him that the entire right side of my face had been swollen, and my right eye was black and blue from the trauma of being born.

Dr. Lundgren asked my mother if he could examine me, and when she said yes, he immediately took me in and ran a simple X-ray of my neck and skull. He developed the X-rays and sat my mother down to show her what he had found. The traumatic birth had dislodged the base of my skull so badly that it was causing interference with the cerebellum and brain stem, which he called a subluxation.

The cerebellum and brain stem are the parts of your brain that are responsible for movement, balance, and equilibrium. Disruption of these areas can definitely cause seizures and present as clinical brain damage. My mother was shocked. Why hadn't the other specialists figured this out?

Dr. Lundgren then asked if he could give me an adjustment to correct the subluxation that was causing a miscommunication between my brain and body. My mother consented, and Dr. Lundgren asked my mother to hold on to my feet. Then he leaned over and cradled my head in his hands, and as my mom held my feet, he performed what is called an occipital lift adjustment.

I remember this loud *pop*, and my eyes flew open like a shot of electricity had just passed through my body. I could feel blood rushing to my head, and it felt like my power was turned back on. I looked over at my mother, and her eyes rolled back in her head, and she collapsed to the ground. Five years of stress had finally caught up to her and caused her to faint. I remember watching Dr. Lundgren calmly walk around the table, softly slap my mom on the face, and tell her that everything was going to be okay. He told her to take me home and throw all the drugs (and that stupid white helmet) in the garbage.

I remember leaving the office and my mother looking over her shoulder to make sure Dr. Lundgren didn't see her put the helmet on my head as we went outside. I remember going home and seeing my mom put the bag of prescription drugs in the cabinet over the fridge, "just in case." I also remember Mom reading to me a few months after that adjustment and how shocked she was when I started reading back to her. I remember being able to read and do math before starting first grade of "normal" school. I also remember excelling in school, playing every possible sport, and only wearing helmets when I absolutely had to!

Dr. Lundgren's adjustment turned my power on, freed up the full potential of my innate intelligence, and allowed me to live life to the fullest. I am now a practicing chiropractic, married to a wonderful woman, who is also a chiropractor, and owe my life to chiropractic care.

Don't Wait for Symptoms to Appear

Unfortunately, our current health-care system is much more focused on symptom relief than the promotion of optimum function leading to health and well-being. As a result, most people wait until they are symptomatic—suffering from a disease—before they report to a doctor for evaluation. Sadly, by the time symptoms appear, the disease is quite advanced. Just think about the deadliest diseases in the world today: heart disease, cancer, stroke, and diabetes. Do any of these diseases display symptoms or warning signs in their early stages? Most cases of these silent killers are incidentally found through routine screening. I am not against routine screening. I firmly believe that early detection of a disease does save lives. However, I also believe that early detection is not synonymous with prevention. What is the medical system today doing to prevent disease?

The medical profession is symptom-based, meaning most diagnoses are made based on the patient's signs and symptoms. As a result, most medical treatment is also symptom-based. This means the treatment is strictly focused on reducing or eliminating the patient's symptoms, which often results in the original cause of the disease being ignored.

Let's use the deadliest of all silent killers, heart disease, as an example. Signs and symptoms of heart disease include high blood pressure and high cholesterol, and typical medical intervention is to chemically drug the system to reduce the blood pressure and cholesterol. Research shows that when a patient discontinues these medications, blood pressure and cholesterol levels not only rise again but also typically elevate to levels even higher than before. However, elevated blood pressure and cholesterol are usually a result of long-term sympathetic (fight-or-flight) dominance. Therefore, taming the Stress Monkey via minor lifestyle changes in the three dimensions of stress and maintaining those changes consistently over time should lower these parameters permanently.

As you will learn later, every spinal subluxation results in a sympathetic (fight-or-flight) response, which, by definition, will raise blood pressure, heart rate, and serum cholesterol. On March 16, 2007, WebMD reported on a placebo-controlled research study that showed that a special chiropractic adjustment can significantly reduce blood pressure in patients with abnormally high blood pressure.

"This procedure has the effect of not one, but two blood-pressure medications given in combination," said study leader George Bakris, MD. "And it seems to be adverse-event free. We saw no side effects and no problems," added Bakris, director of the University of Chicago Hypertension Center. The findings were initially published in the *Journal of Human Hypertension* and then quickly reported on by every major media outlet, including ABC's *Good Morning America*.[2]

Taking this concept one step further, consider not waiting for your blood pressure to stay elevated. Consider implementing these simple and easy lifestyle changes early and before the need arises. We can prevent heart disease, diabetes, and even certain cancers through lifestyle modifications in the three dimensions of stress: physical, biochemical, and psychological. Or, as Dr. Dean Ornish stated, through proper nutrition, exercise, and love.

Please note: If you are currently on medication for a chronic disease, don't stop taking your medication. Ask your doctor to help monitor you as you safely reduce and eventually eliminate the need for the medication.

Medication for chronic conditions should be your last resort. All drugs have side effects, and, if at all possible, they should be avoided. In 2002, *The New England Journal of Medicine* published a study that reported an alarming one in four patients suffered observable side effects from the more than 3.34 billion prescription drugs filled in 2002.[3] On September 27, 2016, *U.S. News and World Report* published an article titled "Death by Prescription." The article states, "By one estimate, taking prescribed medications is the fourth leading cause of death among Americans." The article adds that "estimates dating back nearly two decades put the number at 100,000 or more deaths annually, which includes a study published in the *Journal of the American Medical Association* in 1998 that projected 106,000 deaths." The article further states that recently that number has gone up to 128,000 American deaths per year as a result of taking medications as prescribed.[4]

Notice that this number is not referring to overdose or drug interactions. This is the number of people who die annually in America from taking their medications exactly as prescribed. This number is five times higher than the number of people killed by overdosing on prescription painkillers and heroin.[5] Can you think of any other industry in which 128,000 people die annually as a mere side effect?

If such an industry existed, government officials and industry leaders would be working hard to make changes. Yet in the health-care industry, the only concern expressed by government officials and industry leaders is "How can we give more people access to more medication?" The solution is to work toward eliminating the need for medication by preventing disease and promoting wellness.

Visiting a Chiropractor

How does a chiropractor monitor the health of the nervous system? The most important concept to understand about chiropractic care is that, unlike medicine, the focus of your chiropractic evaluation is not based on your symptoms. In fact, many health-conscious people, including athletes and weekend warriors, regularly visit chiropractors, despite the fact that they have no pain or any other symptoms. Quite often I hear, "Doc, I have no pain or problems. My wife just recommended that I come in and get checked for subluxations."

YOUR FIRST VISIT

The first thing your doctor of chiropractic will do is gather information. This may be done through online health history forms, a face-to-face conversation, or a combination of both.

Next, the chiropractic exam will be focused on looking for the common signs of subluxation. Those signs include postural abnormalities, abnormal heat patterns around the spine, swelling, pain or tenderness to the touch, abnormal muscle tension or spasm, loss of range of motion, and cerebellar dysfunction as determined through abnormal balance and incoordination (clumsiness).

To objectively quantify the effects of subluxation, your chiropractic physician will most likely use computerized instrumentation. Thermography can be used to visualize the abnormal heat patterns around the spine. In a normal and healthy person, the thermal discrepancy on the sides of the spine at each segment will be minimal. For example, the temperature reading to the right of the C1 vertebra (the first bone of the spine just below the skull) should be nearly identical to the temperature on the left side of C1. A warmer reading on one side indicates abnormal blood flow, abnormal constriction, or dilation of blood vessels and signifies that a subluxation exists some-where in the spine (not necessarily at C1).

Electromyography may be used to digitally measure the tension and tone of paraspinal musculature (muscles surrounding the spine). Similar to thermography, muscle tone and tension must be within normal parameters and symmetrical when comparing the right and left at each spinal level. Abnormally high muscle tone indicates mus-cle spasm, while abnormally low tone represents below normal nerve activity and neurological weakness. Both asymmetry of muscle tone and abnormal muscle tone are indications that a subluxation exists somewhere in the spine.

Another computerized test that may be performed on your first visit is digital inclinometry. This is done to accurately measure the range of motion in different regions of the spine. Limited motion, such as the inability to bend at the waist, is an indication of possible subluxation. Similarly, asymmetrical movement patterns (for exam-ple, a person cannot turn his head to the right but has no trouble turning to the left) are indicative of spinal restriction and subluxation. Certainly, instrumentation is not always necessary to see limited range of motion. A visual assessment of how the patient bends and turns will also provide valuable information.

Finally, one of the most useful and revealing computerized tests in chiropractic care is the heart rate variability analysis. The results of this test will provide valuable information regarding the patient's Stress Monkey and her ability to cope with stress. The test will com-pare the patient's stress adaptability to that of the ideally "healthy" person. A low score means the patient will most likely suffer ill health from stressful situations, while a high score indicates that this patient can handle a fair amount of negative stress without succumbing to illness. Furthermore, the heart rate variability test will reveal valuable information about the patient's autonomic nervous system, which automatically controls the blood vessels, glands, and organs.

The heart rate variability test can accurately determine whether a patient is predominantly in the sympathetic or parasympathetic state. Dominance in either system is undesirable. You may want to refer back to the earlier chapters for a list of symptoms that arise from sympathetic or parasympathetic dominance to see if you are balanced or dominant in one system.

In short, if the Stress Monkey is not in balance between the sympathetic and parasympathetic neurological tone, the patient is not healthy—even if he or she has no major pathologies such as diabetes, heart disease, cancer, tumors, or autoimmune disorders. The chiropractic correction of a subluxation has been shown effective in improving heart rate variability and restoring balance in the autonomic nervous system. According to research, "The heart rate variability analysis indicates that chiropractic treatment is associated with a shift to a healthy autonomic nervous system balance."[6]

The typical first visit to the chiropractor is not complete until spinal X-rays have been taken. The X-rays allow the chiropractor to see any spinal abnormality or misalignment that may be present. The X-rays will also reveal the extent of degenerative changes that may have taken place as a result of the subluxation. It may take many years of progressive spinal degeneration before such detrimental changes become visible on an X-ray. Therefore, the X-rays will also allow the chiropractor to estimate the age of the subluxation, which may affect the treatment plan.

DAN'S STORY

Dan was a sixty-year-old retired police officer. He sought my help, because the pain in his lower back was radiating down into his right leg, all the way to his foot. He was also experiencing extreme weakness in the right leg. He needed a cane to get around. He told me that his only grandchild was already a year old, and he never picked her up and held her because of his disability.

After reviewing his X-rays, I informed him that based on the size of the bone spurs and the extent of disc degeneration, this problem had started over twenty years ago and had been gradually progressing during the past twenty years.

Dan had a hard time accepting this. "My pain started last year, not twenty years ago," he said. "Also, my medical doctor said the degeneration in my spine is a normal part of aging, and since I'm getting older, I'm supposed to have arthritis in the spine."

I used the following analogy to address Dan's concern. Imagine you're driving your car and you accidentally hit a pothole. The pothole was so deep that it sounded as though you damaged your car. So you pull over and walk around your car. Everything looks normal. You kick the tires, and they seem fine, so you get back in your car and start driving. There are no abnormal sounds, and the car seems to be driving as before. So you assume everything is okay. However, several thousand miles of driving and months later, you go in for an oil change, and the mechanic says the tires on one side of your car need to be replaced. You may say, "I got all four tires from the same place, at the same time. Why would these two wear out and not the others?" The obvious answer would be that the pothole you hit months ago must have thrown off your alignment. When the alignment is off, the tires wear out unevenly.

How does that apply to the spine? Well, Dan's medical doctor said wear and tear in the spine is a normal part of aging. The degenerative changes in Dan's spine were isolated to two of the discs in his lower back. The other discs looked perfectly healthy. Why would two discs wear out and not the others? Aren't all the discs the same age? Didn't Dan get all his discs from the same place, at the same time?

If degeneration and decay of spinal joints are a normal part of aging, then all the discs and joints in Dan's spine should degenerate, not just two of them. In fact, everyone who is the same age as Dan would have the same exact pattern of degeneration. But, in reality, degeneration and arthritis start at different ages in different people, and they depend mainly on the person's lifestyle stresses, not their age.

So why didn't Dan have pain for the entire twenty years? Why did he begin experiencing pain only over the past one and a half years? For the same reason that your tires don't show signs of misalignment after hitting a pothole, and early stages of cancer have no pain, and heart disease is painless until an artery gets so clogged that the heart can't function anymore.

Fortunately, Dan's story had a happy ending. It took a full year of chiropractic care, but he did regain full function of his right leg without drugs or surgery. Today he is spending most of his retirement playing with his granddaughter.

How would Dan's life have been different if twenty years ago, through a routine wellness visit to his chiropractor, the subluxation had been detected and corrected early? A thermography scan would have shown an abnormal pattern of blood flow around his lower back vertebrae, and an electromyograph would have revealed abnormal muscle tone and asymmetry around the musculature of his lower back. The chiropractor would have then recommended spinal X-rays.

You can probably imagine Dan saying, "But I don't have any back pain. Why should I get X-rays?" Well, if Dan had been routinely checked by his chiropractor before the appearance of symptoms, his problem would have been fixed long before it became symptomatic. Furthermore, he would not have missed an entire year of being able to pick up, hold, and play with his granddaughter.

We know how misalignments can occur in a car, but how do they occur in the spine? As common as hitting a pothole with your car, they can occur during childhood when we're playing in the school-yard or on the monkey bars on the playground. I don't recall anyone being concerned about my spine when I fell off the swing set or crashed my bike as a child. If the bleeding stopped and I was able to move or walk around, then we assumed I was fine.

SUBLUXATIONS

Spinal subluxations can occur around the time a child learns to walk. By the time my youngest son was fifteen months old, he had pretty much mastered walking, but he still fell about every fifteen minutes. How would you feel if you fell every fifteen minutes over the next two hours? How about if you fell five times per day, every day for the next three months? Is it possible there would be a subluxation in your spine? This is why it makes sense to have our children checked by a chiropractor and adjusted on a regular basis.

Spinal subluxations can also result from other trauma, such as car accidents. The forces generated in a car accident are enough to tear ligaments and herniate discs. Certainly, such forces will also result in misalignments of vertebrae and can cause subluxations. Once again, most people are quick to take a pill for their post-accident headache or operate on a herniated disc, but too few people pursue chiropractic care to correct their subluxations after a car accident.

Subluxations are relatively unavoidable at any age. We put pressure on our neck and spine by performing normal activities, such as sitting for a long period of time, performing repetitive movements, lifting, twisting, bending, falling, and so on. Because of this, it is highly improbable that we can avoid misaligning our vertebrae.

Spinal subluxations can even occur during birth. Being born can be very traumatic, especially to the baby's neck. Dr. Ogi Ressel discusses this "largely under-reported" problem in his book *Kids First: Health with No Interference*.[7] "During the process of delivery, there is tremendous stress placed on the head and neck of the baby and often this stress causes vertebral subluxations of the very delicate spinal bones of the infant," states Dr. Ressel.[8]

Vertebral subluxations affect the nervous system and can compromise communication between the brain and the rest of the body. It is particularly important to correct any interference at this stage of life because a newborn is rapidly developing physically, mentally, and neurologically. According to Dr. Ressel, the resulting health problems "can appear seemingly unrelated to the process of delivery and can affect your child months or years later—even as an adult!"[9]

In other words, if communication between the body and the brain is inefficient, then the development of the whole body will be affected. And while some of the problems may be apparent immediately, others may not manifest until much later in life.

Subluxations can cause an array of medical and neurological conditions. Many infant and childhood disorders can be due to subluxations caused at birth or even before that. If the mother's pelvis is misaligned, the baby can be constricted in the womb. This is called in-utero constraint, which means a subluxation of the baby's spine has occurred before birth. Correcting these subluxations is so crucial that it should be part of the medical procedure (like the Apgar screening) for newborns. In his book, Dr. Ressel reports that "certain hospitals in Australia are now having chiropractors check infants immediately after delivery to ensure they have a healthy spine and nervous system free from subluxations."[10] Maybe one day the entire obstetrics community will understand this. However, to date, it is the responsibility of the parents to have their infants checked for subluxations. If not, their infants could manifest any number of issues, including the following:

- Colic
- Feeding problems
- Sleeping disabilities
- Reflux
- Plagiocephaly (flat heads)
- Constipation
- Colds
- Ear infections
- Sinus disorders
- Headaches
- Asthma
- Allergies
- Behavioral disorders
- ADD/ADHD
- Sudden infant death syndrome (SIDS)

And many others.

The experts agree that birth can cause trauma to the brain stem and the upper neck of the baby.[11] Dr. V. Fryman found that 95 percent of 1,250 five-day-old babies had subluxations after birth. These infants also suffered from muscle strain in their neck. Dr. Fryman reported that the babies had immediate muscle relaxation and better sleep after being adjusted.[12] Furthermore, experts agree that constriction of the brain stem and the upper portion of the spinal cord can affect respiration and the respiratory control center of the baby. This negatively affects the baby's ability to breathe properly while asleep. This is how a subluxation resulting from a traumatic birth can cause SIDS.[13]

Too often, a parent's first inclination is to seek out traditional medicine when dealing with childhood health conditions. Unfortunately, the only help they receive is in the way of medications. When an infant is seen by a chiropractor, their subluxations are adjusted manually, and with a very light touch. The results can seem miraculous, and the truth is that once the neurological communication is restored, the body will function at optimal levels.

So let's put it all together. If my spine is subluxated, there is a high probability that I know nothing about it, but while I'm unaware, the subluxation is negatively affecting the inflow of information from the environment to my brain. It is also causing a sympathetic response, which is weakening my immune system, interfering with my ability to rest and sleep, and decreasing my adaptability to stress, resulting in an out-of-control Stress Monkey. Misinformation leads to different patterns of gene expression, which can create more disease and illness and, in turn, lead to a downward health spiral. It is a vicious cycle that continually diminishes my ability to properly respond to stress. This is the classic description of an untamed Stress Monkey.

You cannot prevent subluxations. And, regardless of your age or health status, you can always benefit from chiropractic care. It doesn't matter that you haven't seen a chiropractor recently (or ever); what matters is what you do today. A multitude of health conditions can be rectified, prevented, or at least improved by beginning to take care of your spine. Getting rid of misalignments will improve spinal function and provide you with enormous health benefits. It is the first step in turning stress into strength through a well-disciplined Stress Monkey. Therefore, the most vital and valuable step you should take to tame your Stress Monkey is to get adjusted on a regular basis.

CHAPTER 8

Step Two: Detoxify

*You never know what you have until
you clean your room.*

—Unknown

n Chapter 1, I talk about the fact that your level of health depends
entirely on how much stress you can safely handle. Based on that
fact alone, our focus should be on increasing our body's ability to
handle stress. In other words, we need to tame that Stress Monkey
and teach it to process stress in a way that generates a positive outcome. You learned in the previous two chapters that interference in
the nervous system can and will reduce your ability to handle stress.
Another hinderance in your ability to handle stress can be toxicity.

Dr. Wahls's Story

Dr. Terry Wahls was diagnosed with progressive multiple sclerosis (MS), a debilitating autoimmune disease that led to her requiring a wheelchair within seven years of her diagnosis. In fact, her condition was so bad that she was unable to sit in a chair and had to be reclined in a zero-gravity chair or a tilt wheelchair. All of this happened while she was under the care of the best MS doctors and specialists. But when she started a modern-day hunter-gatherer diet, in three months, she could walk between exam rooms with only one cane while practicing medicine. One month later, she could walk throughout the hospital without a cane. At five months, she got on a bike for the first time in a decade and rode. And at nine months, she rode an eighteen-mile trail on her bike![1]

The Toll of Toxins

You may know someone who catches a cold the minute a breeze blows. Someone else may have stomach issues, and under any amount of stress this person gets acid reflux or indigestion. Another person gets headaches every time something stressful happens. We all know people who are excessively sensitive to stress and easily get depressed, anxious, or angry—and those who succumb to high blood pressure and heart disease the minute life gets difficult. It's a proven fact that people who cannot handle stress have high cortisol levels and are highly likely to develop obesity and type 2 diabetes. These are all examples of people with low stress adaptability. The startling fact is that all the aforementioned people may have toxins in their bodies that are causing them to be weak in the face of stress.

Therefore, after optimizing your Stress Monkey's nervous system through chiropractic care, the next most important area of concern is the elimination of toxins in your environment. Toxins can be found in your food, water, and air. They can enter your body through your nose, mouth, and skin. Let's talk about the most common environmental toxins that you should know about.

Common Environmental Toxins

Heavy metal toxins can be found in drinking water, fish, vaccines, pesticides, antiperspirants, building material, dental amalgams, and manufacturing plants. The common ones are lead, mercury, cadmium, aluminum, and arsenic. They can cause cancer, neurological disorders, Alzheimer's disease, dementia, fatigue, nausea, abnormal heart rhythm, and damage to blood vessels. They have also been closely linked to children with behavioral issues, attention deficit disorder, attention deficit hyperactivity disorder, and autism.

The presence of heavy metal toxins in your body can suppress your immune system, cause autoimmune diseases, and make it very difficult to recover from Lyme disease and other chronic viral infections. Unhealthy skin and gut issues have also been linked to heavy metal toxicity. In short, in the presence of heavy metals, your Stress Monkey becomes powerless. You can't think, fight infections, or digest your food properly.

You may be wondering why lead is still a concern. Isn't all gasoline now unleaded? And hasn't lead paint been outlawed? Both of those things are true, and I'm very glad about that. However, over half of US cities still use lead-lined pipes or copper pipes with lead soldering, which are the primary source of lead in drinking water. To help combat this, make sure you are drinking only pure water. Many old houses still have lead-based paint on the walls. Lead in the body causes high blood pressure, heart attacks, kidney damage, reproductive dysfunction, and strokes. In children it can cause delayed neurological and physical development.

Arsenic is a well-known poison and is classified as a human carcinogen by the Environmental Protection Agency. That means arsenic is likely to cause cancer in humans. It accumulates in the body, and in pregnant women it can cross the placenta and affect the fetus. Similar to lead, it can be found in water. It enters the water supply from smelting of ores such as copper and iron. High levels of arsenic will cause cardiovascular disease and abnormal fetal development.

Also, like lead and arsenic, cadmium can be found in water. Soft and acidic water can cause cadmium to be leached out of pipes. It can also enter the water supply from leaking landfills and fertilizer runoff. Cadmium is also present in large quantities in cigarette smoke. It damages the lung tissue and builds up over time to cause kidney, liver, bone, and blood damage. If you are a smoker and are having a hard time handling stress in your life, one of the best things you can do for yourself is quit smoking. It will do wonders for your Stress Monkey.

Mercury is the most common toxic heavy metal. It is also one of the most dangerous toxins out there. It is present in fish, the air we breathe, and dental amalgam (fillings). It has also been added as a preservative to many vaccines. Many experts believe that most people have elevated levels of mercury in their bodies. Since it is a strong neurotoxin (toxic to the nervous system), exposure to mercury can cause tremors, mood swings, irritability, nervousness, insomnia, weakness, numbness, pain, twitching, headaches, disturbances in sensation, and poor mental function. Higher levels of exposure can cause kidney failure, respiratory failure, and death.[2]

There are many other toxic heavy metals, but I have chosen to discuss only the ones that are most prevalent in our environment today. The last of these is aluminum, which is found in antacids, dyes, cake mix, processed cheese, deodorants, antiperspirants, baking soda/

powder, foil, cookware, vaccines, shampoos, cosmetics, lotions, soda cans, soy-based baby formulas, and lactose-intolerant baby formulas. As you can see, the list is quite extensive. Some experts say that aluminum cookware and soda cans are perfectly safe, but there is a lot of controversy around the aluminum in deodorants, antiperspirants, and vaccines. Aluminum has been linked to dementia and Alzheimer's disease.[3] It is also linked to epilepsy, osteomalacia, attention deficit disorder, and chronic fatigue syndrome.

A quick search on the internet will provide you with practical ways to avoid aluminum in your environment. For example, you can use glass pans for baking, stoneware for cookie sheets, and cast iron for stove-top cooking. Also, reduce the number of times you cook food wrapped in foil. Look for natural, aluminum-free deodorants and baking soda. Avoid antacids and look for natural remedies for heartburn. There are plenty of them on the internet. I recommend a tablespoon of organic apple cider vinegar diluted in a couple ounces of water.

Other environmental toxins are pesticides, which are found in bug sprays and commercially raised meats and produce. Pesticides can cause cancer, Parkinson's disease, miscarriages, nerve damage, and birth defects. To avoid this toxin, do your best to get your meats and produce from certified organic farms. Also, don't ingest any bug spray.

No, we're not done! Phthalates are found in plastic wrap, plastic bottles, and other plastic food containers. Phthalates can wreak havoc on your endocrine system. Specifically, they disturb the estrogen and testosterone balance in the body. In women it can cause an increase in the harmful type of estrogen that can lead to breast cancer. In men it can cause a significant decline in testosterone, which will lead to weight gain, muscle loss, and erectile dysfunction. Reduce your use of plastic containers, and do your best to never microwave food in plastic containers. Use glassware if you have to use the microwave.

Then there is asbestos. Asbestos was used between 1950 and the 1970s. It can still be found in insulation material in flooring, ceilings, water pipes, and heating ducts. It is common knowledge that asbestos will cause severe scarring in lung tissue and cause a deadly cancer called mesothelioma. Visit www.asbestos.com for more information.

Chlorine is found in common household cleaners, swimming pools, and drinking water. It can cause sore throat, coughing, eye irritation, rapid breathing, wheezing, pain in the lungs, and lung collapse. It can also cause cancer. To avoid chlorine, drink purified water and use organic detergents and household cleaners. If you are planning to install a pool in your home, consider a saltwater pool.

As if all of that wasn't toxic enough, the list goes on and on. There is cyanide in insecticides, nitrates and nitrogen fertilizers that get in water, dioxins, solvents such as benzene, Polychlorinated Biphenyls (PCBs), radioactive materials, and fluoride. There is a lot of debate as to whether fluoride in water is harmful. My personal opinion is that it should be avoided. However, I encourage you to do your own research on this matter.

Activate Your Immune System

If you're anything like me, looking at the previous list of endless toxic possibilities in your environment has made you feel a bit overwhelmed. Good! Because that allows me to make a point. It is impossible to avoid toxins, just as it is impossible to not face stress in your life. What should we do? Avoidance of toxins should not be abandoned and should be part of your strategy, but more important is boosting your immune system and supporting your internal detoxification pathways. The good news is that your body comes with some standard equipment that naturally detoxifies and cleans your internal and cellular environment.

In the same way that toxins can cause disease pathways to be activated, there are natural substances and foods that will activate detoxification in your body. One of those foods is cilantro. In an article titled "12 Cilantro Benefits, Nutrition and Recipes," Rachael Link explains how this one herb can powerfully aid in detoxifying your body.[4] She states, "Cilantro . . . has been shown to bind these toxic metals together, loosening them from tissue, and facilitating their elimination from the body." According to the article, other benefits of cilantro are as follows: It protects against oxidative stress, lowers anxiety, improves sleep, lowers blood sugar levels, protects against cardiovascular disease, prevents urinary tract infections, settles digestive upset, protects against food poisoning, supports healthy menstrual function, prevents neurological inflammation, protects against colon cancer, and soothes skin irritations.

So what was Dr. Wahls's diet protocol for overcoming MS? On a daily basis, she ate three cups of green leafy vegetables, three cups of sulfur-rich vegetables, and three cups of color vegetables. (One great way to help your body rid itself of accumulated toxins is by eating sulfur-rich foods.) Dr. Wahls, a medical doctor, has written extensively about the benefits of these foods. Also included in her diet in smaller amounts were grass-fed meat, organ meats, and seaweed. Her full plan is described in her book *Minding My Mitochondria: How I Overcame Secondary Progressive Multiple Sclerosis (MS) and Got out of My Wheelchair*.

She has also written a best seller titled *The Wahls Protocol*. In this book, she states that the liver and kidneys need sulfur to remove toxins from the bloodstream.[5] Here is a list of sulfur-rich foods that she recommends: cabbage, broccoli, cauliflower, brussels sprouts, onion, garlic, mushrooms, and asparagus. If you include these in your daily diet, the stress of environmental toxins will not be as detrimental on your body. Dr. Wahls also recommends that you eat seaweed at least once per week. Seaweed also has powerful toxin-removal properties, especially with respect to mercury, lead, and other heavy metals.

At this point, you may be asking, "What about detoxification regimens?" I am a fan of detoxing, but I don't have a particular plan that I recommend. There are many to choose from, and you should pick one that suits your lifestyle and matches your abilities. There are detox programs that require long hours or multiple days of fasting. If you have a hard time fasting, you may want to choose a different plan. You may want to explore Dr. Josh Axe's book *Bone Broth Breakthrough*.[6] Bone broth can be of tremendous help during detoxification, because it can help rehydrate your body while also supporting your liver's production of essential nutrients. Bone broth contains minerals that the body needs. During times of fasting, it will allow for fat loss while preserving muscle tissue, because it has protein-sparing properties.

If you are interested in detoxification, Dr. Josh Axe's book *Eat Dirt* is a great starting point.[7] In this book, Dr. Axe talks about the detoxifying properties of clay and charcoal. Now you know why he called it *Eat Dirt*. Activated charcoal is used by poison control centers to remove poisonous material from the body, and clay can also trap toxins to expel them.

One final thought: Consider also taking probiotics as a part of your regular supplement regimen. Probiotics are microorganisms or bacteria that live in your digestive tract. They help you digest your food by producing enzymes that break down food and "junk" that may have gotten into your intestines. They can also facilitate heavy metal removal through the intestines. If you have had a course of antibiotics in the past, chances are that the antibiotics didn't kill just the bad bugs. They probably also wiped out the good bacteria.

When deciding which brand of probiotics to purchase, I like to make sure the label on the bottle reads something to the effect of 2.5 (or more) billion viable cells. The count ensures that you are getting the right dose of probiotics, and the words "viable cells" mean the bacteria are alive, which is what you want. The higher-quality brands will also require that you keep the bottle refrigerated to keep the little creatures alive.

In summary, our world is filled with toxins and harmful material. It is nearly impossible to avoid them. Do your best to reduce your exposure to them by drinking pure water, not storing your food in plastics, eating organic meats and produce, and using organic deodorants, detergents, and cosmetics. Eat a lot of cilantro, sulfur-rich vegetables, and colorful fruits, and take probiotics. Also consider reading the books I recommended. If you reduce your exposure to toxins, boost your immune system, and support the detoxifying organs in your body, you will allow your Stress Monkey to focus on helping you realize your dreams and build the life that you want and deserve.

CHAPTER 9

Step Three: Get Some Sun

We can easily forgive a child who is afraid of the dark;
the real tragedy of life is when men are afraid of the light.

—Plato, *The Republic*

The environment is critical to proper healthy gene expression. Once your nervous system has been evaluated and optimized through chiropractic care and you have hopefully begun the process of reducing or eliminating any dependency on medication, the next step is to work on creating the perfect outside environment. That process begins with light.

The Benefits of Sunlight

I'm speaking about natural sunlight. In our current culture we have been taught that sunlight exposure is unhealthy. Television and internet advertisements, as well as public service announcements, are full of warnings about how sunlight may cause wrinkles and skin cancer. Such claims are simply not true. Research shows that spending time in the sun is one of the most powerful methods of fighting disease. This research shows that sunlight can help us prevent illnesses such as the following:

- Heart disease
- Cancer
- Autoimmune disorders
- Asthma
- Digestive disorders
- Painful conditions such as fibromyalgia

This information is best explained in the book *Dark Deception* by Dr. Joseph Mercola.[1] I strongly urge you to read this book. Dr. Mercola does an excellent job of comparing current research with common medical practice to reveal the myth about sun exposure. One of the startling facts he talks about is that sunlight will actually reduce your risk of cancer, while most commercial sunscreen lotions actually increase the risk of skin cancer.

I am not saying that sunlight cannot cause skin damage. Anyone who has had a sunburn knows that the rays of the sun are full of energy and that anything healthy can also be harmful in excess. A sunburn can certainly trigger the onset of skin cancer, but there is no evidence that sun exposure that does not result in a burn will have the same effect. According to the American Academy of Dermatology, a "blistering sunburn during childhood or adolescence can nearly double a person's chance of developing melanoma" later in life.[2] Therefore, to be safe, keep your sun exposure to twenty minutes or less. Also, keep in mind that the sun's rays are the most intense between 11:00 a.m. and 3:00 p.m. So the best time of day to sunbathe or partake in outdoor activities would be before 11:00 a.m. or later in the evening.

In his book, Dr. Mercola states that there is no evidence that sunscreens actually prevent melanoma. In fact, he cites research that states populations in higher latitudes where there is less sunlight have a higher prevalence of melanoma. Meanwhile, those who spend more time in the sun tend to have a lower probability of developing melanoma. "Careful sunbathing has the potential to radically reduce many of the chronic degenerative diseases that rank among the greatest health problems faced by modern man," states Dr. Mercola.[3]

The basis for such claims is the fact that the body produces vitamin D when the skin is exposed to sunlight. According to an article published in *The American Journal of Clinical Nutrition*, as little as ten minutes of sun exposure per day may be enough to prevent vitamin D deficiency. Apparently, many other experts agree with Dr. Mercola, because their research also suggests that vitamin D may provide protection from osteoporosis, hypertension (high blood pressure), cancer, and several autoimmune diseases.[4] In case you are wondering what autoimmune diseases are, here are some examples:

- Multiple sclerosis
- Type 1 diabetes
- Rheumatoid arthritis
- Psoriasis
- Lupus

- Inflammatory bowel diseases such as the following:
  · Crohn's disease
  · Ulcerative colitis

In his book, Dr. Mercola also states that vitamin D produced as a result of exposure to sunlight may prevent the devastating effects of Alzheimer's disease.

So why am I insisting that we get our vitamin D from the sun instead of just taking vitamin D supplements? First, anything accomplished naturally is far superior to its synthetic counterpart. Second, there are potentially dangerous side effects that can result from an overdose of vitamin D taken orally. Those side effects are rare but mainly include abnormally high blood calcium levels that can cause kidney stones and bone pain. Vitamin D toxicity also causes nausea, vomiting, weakness, and frequent urination. The human body is able to self-regulate, and it is highly unlikely that the body will produce toxic doses of vitamin D as a result of sunbathing.

On the other hand, taking vitamin D supplements requires that you closely monitor your blood vitamin D levels through laboratory testing to ensure proper dosing. Keep in mind that some synthetic vitamin D supplements have been proven ineffective, which makes them a complete waste of money.

Sunlight and Serotonin

If that isn't enough reason to spend moderate amounts of time in the sun, consider the fact that sunlight also helps the body regulate its natural mood-stabilizing hormones and neurotransmitters such as serotonin. Serotonin is the body's natural antidepressant. According to a WebMD article published on December 5, 2002, "A new study shows that the brain produces more of the mood-lifting chemical serotonin on sunny days than on darker days."[5] In this article, the researchers state that the level of serotonin in the blood was directly related to the number of hours of sunlight in the day.

Combine that information with the fact that most antidepressant medication works to increase serotonin levels in the body. Some antidepressant drugs block the reuptake to serotonin after it has been released, and others block the breakdown of serotonin. The problem is that all antidepressants have serious side effects. In fact, the Mayo Clinic warns us that the "Food and Drug Administration (FDA) requires that all antidepressants carry black box warnings, the strictest warnings for prescriptions." That's because many people, especially those under the age of twenty-five, have noticed a serious increase in suicidal thoughts and behaviors after starting antidepressants.[6]

It only makes sense to allow your body to naturally increase serotonin levels through exposure to sunlight as opposed to risking the side effects of medication. So if the stress in your life is causing depression, and your physician has recommended or prescribed an antidepressant, it is worth spending some time in the sun for a few days before resorting to taking the medication. Also, it is strictly critical that if you are already taking an antidepressant, do not stop taking it without discussing this with your physician. Some antidepressants can have severe withdrawal symptoms, and you may need to gradually reduce your dosage over time. Also, suddenly stopping antidepressants can cause a dramatic increase in depression. It is perfectly safe to spend fifteen to twenty minutes in the sun even if you are on an antidepressant.

The suggestions I give you in this book are practical, easy to implement into your daily life, and do not require much additional time out of your schedule. You may not have the time to spend fifteen minutes sunbathing every day, for example, or you may live in a climate that has limited hours of sunlight and you may not have the resources to migrate south for the winter every year. So let's talk about the practical applications of this information and how we can get more exposure to sunlight in a safe manner.

One quick way to increase healthy sunlight exposure is to not wear sunglasses.[7] Obviously, looking directly at the sun is terribly detrimental to your eyes. Also, glasses will protect your eyes from flying debris when riding a motorcycle or in a convertible car. So take the necessary precautions. However, if you are walking from your car to your office, in the parking lot of a grocery store, or going out to check the mail, it's a good idea not to wear sunglasses. We absorb a high level of the sunlight we need through our eyes. Unfortunately, glass and plastic both block 100 percent of the ultraviolet rays of the sun. Whenever possible, wear shorts and short-sleeve shirts and try not to cover your face when going outside. Do not wear sunscreens, unless you are going to be in the sun for an extended period of time (longer than twenty minutes), and be sure to use natural organic sunscreens. Dr. Mercola's book *Dark Deception* is an excellent reference for sunscreen information.

Finally, if none of the preceding suggestions are practical for you, here is one last option to improve your natural vitamin D and serotonin levels. Use full-spectrum lighting at home or in your office. Full-spectrum light bulbs are easy to find. Typically, full-spectrum light bulbs come in the form of fluorescent bulbs or tubes. A search on the internet can quickly help you find a desk lamp that provides you with full-spectrum lighting. Always have a full-spectrum lamp on your desk when working. If possible, change all the light bulbs in your home to full-spectrum light bulbs. Nothing artificial will ever fully replace the real thing, but natural-spectrum light lamps can be a safe alternative.

How does this benefit your Stress Monkey? First off, your Stress Monkey has a tendency to overreact to stress by overactivating the fight-or-flight syndrome. Over time, this can lead to high blood pressure and high cholesterol levels. The precursor to vitamin D is cholesterol. In fact, if you look at the molecular structure of cholesterol next to vitamin D, you will see great similarity. Your skin, when exposed to sunlight, can convert excess cholesterol into vitamin D. Furthermore, the mood-stabilizing neurotransmitter serotonin can work wonders in keeping your Stress Monkey calm during times of distress.

Under long-term distress the body releases cortisol. High levels of cortisol sustained over time lead to excessive wear and tear in the body, increased abdominal fat, and osteoporosis. Vitamin D can counteract this process by maintaining healthy bones, joints, and other tissues.

When serotonin levels are normal, your Stress Monkey is much less likely to overreact to your fears and worries. Quite often clinical depression is caused by lowered serotonin levels, and a majority of antidepressant medication is designed to raise your levels of serotonin. How much happier will you be if you actively reduce your chances of depression by naturally increasing serotonin?

CHAPTER 10

Step Four: Visualize

Whatever the mind of man can
conceive and believe, it can achieve.

—W. Clement Stone, *The Success System That Never Fails*

T he biggest difference between the ultrahealthy and the unhealthy may very well be the way they think. Every thought manifests in a physiological response in the body. Just close your eyes and visualize your favorite food on a silver platter in front of you. Even if you weren't really hungry, you may begin to feel a little hunger. Now visualize picking up a lime, cutting it into slices, picking up one of the slices, sinking your teeth deep into it, and allowing the lime juice to pour into your mouth. If you played along and really visualized the lime in your mouth, you're most likely salivating right now. That's what I mean when I say your mental images will manifest as physical responses in your body.

What we dream about and visualize has a major effect in our bodies. That effect can be positive, or it can be negative. Focus on your fears and worries, and your body will behave as if your worst nightmares have come true. Worrying is intentionally visualizing terrifying things. Dreaming with positive intentions is visualizing wonderful things. One will irritate and agitate your Stress Monkey, and the other will empower, energize, and motivate your Stress Monkey.

Tom's Story

In his audiobook *Goals: How to Set Them, How to Reach Them*, motivational speaker Zig Ziglar tells the story of Tom Hartman, a man who attended one of his seminars. Mr. Ziglar received a letter from Tom describing his story. In the letter, Tom wrote that, at first, he was extremely skeptical and wanted to leave the seminar, believing this was just another motivational speech. At the time, Tom weighed 407 pounds and had a 63.5-inch waistline. He had attempted to lose weight many times, claimed to have tried every diet on the planet, and was still unsuccessful. By the end of the seminar, he had a glimmer of hope that a transformation was possible. He borrowed money and purchased the audio cassettes of Zig Ziglar's seminar. He listened to the seminar over and over, so much that he had the seven-hour program memorized. Even then, he continued to listen to it daily, and through all the repetition he began to believe the information being taught.

After a period of time, he found that not only had his eating habits changed but so had his thoughts and desires. The lifestyle choices he was making caused him to lose over one hundred pounds with relatively little effort. He was still significantly overweight, but now he was able to perform his daily activities and run errands independently. One day he was in the grocery store pushing his shopping cart when a little boy at the end of the aisle exclaimed, "Mommy, look at the fat man." The embarrassed mother tried to hush and move the young boy along but could not keep him from pointing directly at Tom. However, Tom found himself turning from side to side searching for the enormous man that the little boy was fascinated by. It took him a moment to realize that the little boy had been pointing directly at him.

In his letter Tom said, "That was so funny, I laughed until I literally cried and for the first time in my adult life I knew that I was going to survive." Tom was thrilled to realize that his image of himself had changed so drastically that he no longer viewed himself as fat. Even though he still weighed over three hundred pounds, he was no longer obese, because he didn't see himself that way. He credits the audio program with reprogramming his mind and helping him change his self-image. He believes that the reason he was able to lose weight was that he had created a new mental identity for himself in which he was thin. It was only his body that had to catch up to that image, and it was doing just that.

Zig Ziglar goes on to explain that when we have a self-image that is obese, we may work hard and lose weight but then go to sleep and dream as an obese person. We go to work and behave as an obese person. We socialize with our friends in the manners of an obese person. "The body works to complete the picture that the mind has given it," states Mr. Ziglar. Tom went on to weigh just over two hundred pounds, which is good for someone who is six foot three. He has also created success in other areas of his life. In conclusion, Mr. Ziglar says that Tom used to be "physically, spiritually, socially, and financially bankrupt, yet because he got involved in the development of a good self-image, he was able to achieve great things, and the results were absolutely spectacular."[1]

Just like Tom Hartman, you can use visualization to clarify your own self-image. How do you see yourself when you're not standing in front of a mirror? Do you see yourself as a powerful, magnificent creation of God? How you see yourself in your mind is how you will always be. Bob Proctor, the famous author and speaker on personal development, likens the self-image to a thermostat. If you set your thermostat to seventy degrees and the temperature in your house drops to sixty-eight, the furnace will kick on, heat will be generated, and the temperature in your home will begin to rise. Then, when the temperature reaches seventy degrees, the furnace will automatically turn off. In the same way, your self-image is the thermostat of how you look. If you work hard and lose some weight, your body will begin to work toward regaining that weight, and eventually your weight will return to its original setting.

Find out what motivates you and focus on that. Do not allow negativity, fear, doubt, and worry to enter your mind. Visualize yourself as you would like to be. Then focus on that image regularly and consistently. Spend sixty to ninety seconds multiple times per day visualizing yourself the way you want to be, and do this until you begin to believe that the image is real. When you believe in your mind and heart that the new self-image is real, then you know that you have reset your thermostat, and you will begin to see permanent changes. Dr. Wayne Dyer wrote a book called *You Will See It When You Believe It*. Well, the title says it all. Most of us go through life saying the exact opposite, that we will believe it when we see it, but with regard to changing your physical body, you must first believe it before you will ever see it.

Visualization as a Tool

When dealing with psychological stress, few tools are easier to use than visualization. This technique will have a significant impact in the physical and biochemical dimensions of stress as well. Visualization is a type of meditation. In an article titled "Meditation: A Simple, Fast Way to Reduce Stress," the Mayo Clinic states, "Meditation can give you a sense of calm, peace and balance that benefits both your emotional well-being and your overall health. And these benefits don't end when your meditation session ends. Meditation can help carry you more calmly through your day and can even improve certain medical conditions."[2] The same article by the Mayo Clinic states that some research suggests that meditation can help with common conditions such as the following:

- Allergies
- Anxiety disorders
- Asthma
- Binge eating
- Cancer
- Depression
- Fatigue
- Heart disease
- High blood pressure
- Pain
- Sleep problems
- Substance abuse

It's important to remember that meditation is not a treatment of any specific condition. Meditation is a tool that will increase and improve your ability to handle stress in the three dimensions of life: physical, biochemical, and psychological. It is a powerful tool that can be very useful when taming your Stress Monkey.

Understandably, the term "meditation" can be intimidating to some people, and it may seem more complicated than it should be. A simple visualization exercise may take less than sixty seconds to accomplish. For example, just imagine yourself on vacation. In your mind, return to a place where you experienced some of your fondest memories, and relive those moments. Remember who was with you and what it felt like to be there. Remember the sights and scenery. Remember the sounds and the smells.

Close your eyes and pretend that you have actually gone back to your favorite place. If it's the beach that you like, then pretend you can hear the waves crashing and seagulls squawking. Pretend you can feel the breeze in your hair and feel the sun on your face.

You may also choose to go somewhere you've never been. You may want to climb K2 or hike the Appalachian Trail. You can go island hopping in the Caribbean or scuba diving in the South Pacific. You can play golf on the world's most exotic golf courses. You can go one-on-one with Michael Jordan or score the winning goal in the World Cup Championship game. Even the sky isn't the limit. You can go to outer space or other planets.

Set a timer for one minute and begin visualizing. Try it right now. After sixty seconds, return from your virtual vacation feeling refreshed and rested. Do this exercise at least once per day, and on more stressful days, you can do this every hour if you like. The only requirement is that you make it as real as possible. You must visualize every imaginable detail while on your virtual vacation. It has to feel as if you are really there. Also, during this sixty-second vacation, you are not allowed to think about work, emails, bills, meetings, or appointments. Just tell yourself they will be waiting for you when you're done and that you'll attend to them then. The health benefits of this exercise are extraordinary, and, as I promised earlier, it hardly requires any time out of your schedule.

Research shows that the mind cannot tell the difference between an actual event experienced and one that is vividly imagined in detail. That explains the detrimental effects of fear and worry. Worry is negative visualization. It's you imagining the worst-case scenario. It is you living out in your mind something awful in vivid detail. And since your brain cannot tell the difference between something actually happening and something that is imagined, it makes the body act as if it is actually happening. That is exactly how people can worry themselves sick. The same hormones get released and the same physiological response will take place as if this negative event that you are worried about is actually happening.

In one experiment, the subjects of the research study were asked to lift an object while electromyography was used to measure muscle fiber recruitment. Then the subjects were asked to imagine that the object they were lifting was much heavier. The result was that more muscle fibers were activated when the subject imagined lifting a heavier weight. In other words, the person lifted the same weight but imagined that it was much heavier, and his muscles got stronger. In the same study, muscle recruitment was measured while the subject only imagined lifting a weight. The result was similar to when the person actually lifted the weight. Furthermore, the researchers found that imagining lifting a heavier object resulted in more electromyogram activity than imagining lifting a light weight. In conclusion, visualization resulted in stronger brain activation and higher muscle excitation.[3]

In another study, the wrists and hands of healthy individuals were immobilized for four weeks to induce weakness and atrophy in their forearm muscles. The subjects were divided into two groups, and one group was asked to visualize strong muscle contractions in their wrists and hands for five days per week, while the other group did nothing. After the four-week period, everyone's wrist strength was measured. The group that did nothing displayed a loss in strength of about 40 to 50 percent, meaning their wrists were only half as strong as before. The group that performed the mental activity of visualizing hand and wrist contractions only displayed a loss in strength of about 18 to 29 percent. Just by using their imagination, they were able to slow down muscle and strength loss.[4] In fact, thirty-seven different research studies conducted between 1995 and 2018 all reveal that mental practice and visualization have an "enduring positive influence on performance."[5]

The benefits of visualization go beyond improving muscle strength and tone. Visualization has been shown to improve coordination, timing, and speed.[6] This was demonstrated by studying two groups of expert pianists. One group performed mental visualization, while the other group physically practiced a challenging music sequence. The results showed that visualization improved movement accuracy and speed, as well as optimized movement timing. In other words, visualization and mental practice improved not only strength and speed but also muscle coordination. Based on all the research, it is no wonder why high-level athletes believe in the power of visualization.

Is there an area in your life where you could benefit from increased strength, speed, and accuracy? Begin visualizing. If visualization is this powerful in athletic performance, it will certainly work wonders for you in managing stress. Instead of visualizing your worst nightmares, visualize your dreams coming true. Visualize winning a prize and enjoying it. Visualize getting a promotion at work and feeling the joy. Visualize your body in the shape you dream it would be.

Dr. Bernie Siegel is the author of several books, including the famous best seller *Love, Medicine and Miracles.*[7] In this book he writes about his experience as a general and pediatric surgeon, as well as his vast experience working with thousands of cancer patients. Dr. Siegel was able to accomplish miraculous results in cancer patients through visualization techniques. Patients who were expected to die within a few weeks of being diagnosed with cancer were able to survive and continue a productive life for many years, thanks in part to Dr. Siegel's visualization techniques.

Dr. Siegel used imagery to assess the mental state of his cancer patients. When working with children, he would ask them to draw a picture of their disease, or a picture of their doctors, nurses, or treatment methods, and so on. Through these experiments, Dr. Siegel discovered that the pictures the kids drew could be used as an indicator or even a predictor of how they would respond to their treatments. For example, if a child drew a skull-and-bones symbol on the radiation therapy equipment, it meant that the child had a negative view of his or her therapy and probably was not handling the stress of his or her illness in an effective manner. On the other hand, if the child drew angel wings on the treating doctor and nurse, you could tell this child was hopeful about his or her recovery and probably would respond positively to the doctor's care. Dr. Siegel would then use the child's imagination and visualization techniques to improve their internal picture and their ability to handle the stress they were under.

Dr. Siegel's books are full of emotionally charged and inspiring stories of how his patients were able to overcome serious health challenges through such techniques. His books will also provide you with tools and examples of different types of visualization and meditations you can use in the convenience of your home. I highly recommend that you begin by reading *Love, Medicine and Miracles.*

Our brains are capable of conducting simulations that are far more complicated than any computer. Have you ever had a dream or nightmare that seemed real? People have reported waking up from a nightmare drenched in sweat or feeling tired, as if they had actually been running. Others have reported having sore muscles after waking from a dream in which they performed physically strenuous activity. Once again, this proves that the human mind is more powerful than we can imagine. The mind has healing power that is not always utilized by those who need it the most. Don't wait until life stress causes illness in your body. Use daily sixty-second visualizations to increase your body's adaptability to stress so that your stress becomes a stimulus for making you stronger and healthier. And if you do encounter an illness, use visualization tools to improve your health.

There is a condition called medical student syndrome. It refers to medical students who experience the symptoms of a disease they are studying. It is also known by other names, such as medical students' disease, second year syndrome, intern's syndrome, or medicalstudentitis. In an article published by the Canadian Medical Association titled "Imagined Illnesses Can Cause Real Problems for Medical Students," the author states, "Although some might consider medical school syndrome trivial, even comical, mental health experts insist it's no joke."[8]

I remember asking my professors to order an MRI for me, because I was convinced that I had MS. Studying the disease and learning about the intricacies of how it can affect your nervous system made me start to actually experience the symptoms I was reading about. The same thing happened when I was studying hepatitis; I literally thought my skin was turning yellow. I firmly believe that the human mind has the power to manifest symptoms of any disease. If by studying, focusing on, and constantly thinking about a disease we can begin to experience symptoms, then perhaps it's possible to manifest symptoms of health, wellness, and vitality by studying and focusing on wellness. Is it possible that you're actually getting healthier simply by reading this book? Dr. Joe Dispenza, the author of several books, including *Breaking the Habit of Being Yourself: How to Lose Your Mind and Create a New One*, teaches that if the mind has the power to make you sick, it only makes sense that it also has the power to make you well.[9]

CHAPTER 11

Step Five: Move Your Body

Life is like riding a bicycle. To keep
your balance, you must keep moving.

—Albert Einstein, to his son Eduard, 1930

I n the fall of 2008 at a wellness conference in Chicago, a lady spoke about her drastic health transformation. I don't remember her name or any other details about her, but I do remember her inspiring story. She started by saying that within the past twelve months, she had lost over one hundred pounds of weight. Her blood pressure was down, her blood sugar was normal, and she no longer felt tired all the time. When the large crowd of doctors had finished clapping, she revealed her motivation: Her only sister had passed away a year ago. She died because she was obese and had many health issues related to obesity. Sadly, she was the single mother of three little children, who were now orphaned. Our presenter stated that she was the children's last living relative and wanted to be the one to provide them with a loving home. She also realized that if she didn't improve her health, she would soon follow in her sister's footsteps and pass away. She decided that these children didn't deserve another tragic loss. So she made the decision to exercise, eat right, and live the wellness lifestyle. She went to work with a great deal of motivation and determination, and one year later she looked and felt amazing. The audience members rose to their feet and gave her a huge standing ovation.

Life is motion, and being motionless is equivalent to death. It is important to incorporate motion into your daily life. Ideally, you should exercise for thirty to forty-five minutes per day, but I also want to make sure that anything I recommend will not require a great amount of resources such as time and money. Therefore, let's discuss ways to include movement in your life. Any movement is beneficial.

Incorporate Movement into Your Daily Life

Here are some simple ideas:

- Take the stairs instead of the elevator whenever possible.
- Park at the far end of the parking lot and force yourself to walk farther when you go shopping.
- If you work at a desk in an office building, drink enough water so you have to go to the restroom every couple of hours. Then, go to the farthest restroom, preferably on a different floor, and take the stairs.
- Move as much as you can, as often as you can.

If your life is already hectic, then finding extra time to force-fit a forty-five-minute workout can actually cause more harm than good. Especially if that involves a fifteen-minute commute each way to the gym, time to socialize with your gym buddies, and then time to shower and get cleaned up. A forty-five-minute workout can actually take close to two hours out of your schedule.

If exercise is something you want to commit to doing daily, you must make it easy to fit into your life. Imagine if brushing your teeth required over an hour to do each day. Would you really do it twice a day, every day? If brushing teeth were that time-consuming, I think more people would resort to dentures. However, I wouldn't visualize that one!

Perhaps that's not a very realistic example, but consider why most people don't eat a healthy and well-balanced breakfast every day. It is because they don't have time to prepare it. That's why we tend to resort to the unhealthy choices, such as cereal or granola bars. It is possible that some cereals and some granola bars can be somewhat healthy (depending on your definition of healthy), but they are not healthy replacements for breakfast.

In the same way, a short three-minute workout before your morning shower may not be the most ideal and healthy scenario, but it is always better than no exercise at all. So let's discuss three-minute options for daily exercise.

Rhythmic, repetitive exercises will not only benefit your cardiovascular system but also help synchronize your biorhythms. Everything in your body runs on cycles and has a rhythm. Negative stress in its three forms (physical, chemical, and psychological) will wreak havoc on those biological rhythms and bring out the worst in your Stress Monkey. For example, you'll notice that the minute you become emotionally stressed, your breathing rhythm will alter, and you may even hold your breath. So consider doing rhythmic, repetitive exercises such as jumping rope or hula hooping. Spend just three minutes in the morning jumping rope. Don't take any breaks. You can rest after your three minutes.

Set your stopwatch and begin. Don't stop until the three minutes are up. Jumping jacks are not as beneficial, but if you don't have rope and you don't have a hoop, they are the next best thing. The only requirement is that the exercise must have a rhythm to it.

Another example would be doing a dance sequence over and over to a three-minute song. Play your favorite dance song and do something repetitive for three minutes. The only stipulation is you must stay on the beat.

Other three-minute exercise options include exercises that build strength and coordination. Suggestions would be push-ups, pull-ups, lunges, and squats. Your entire workout could be seeing how many push-ups you can do in three minutes. Aim high! You can purchase an inexpensive pull-up bar that fastens to a doorframe to do pull-up exercises. Use a chair to assist you if you cannot do full pull-ups on your own. The next day you can count how many squats you can do in three minutes, and another day you can do lunges for three minutes. Keep track of how many you did, and work to increase your repetitions with each workout.

Isometric exercises will also be of great benefit to your health. Isometrics are exercises during which the joints don't move and the muscle length does not change. You simply hold a difficult position for as long as you can. Examples include wall squats and the abdominal plank exercise. There are several variations of each of these exercises. For example, wall squats can be made easier or more difficult by changing the angle of your knees. The more advanced person can do single-leg wall squats or weighted wall squats, where you hold a set of heavy dumbbells in your hands during the exercise. Your entire workout would be to hold a certain position for the entire three minutes.

In addition to the preceding exercises, you can choose your favorite yoga pose and hold that for three minutes or get into a deep martial arts stance and hold that for three minutes. Be sure to choose a position or exercise that is difficult for you. It should be something that initially you can hold for only one minute, and you should challenge yourself to be able to do it for the entire three minutes. Then make the exercise harder, and shoot for three minutes again.

You will notice that I didn't go into much detail on the specific exercises and how to perform each one. This is because this book is not on how to exercise. It is about taming your Stress Monkey. There are countless credible books and magazines on the subject of exercise and fitness. There are gyms that offer exercise classes, and there are personal trainers who would be happy to help you learn more about the human body with respect to exercise. Even a simple search on the internet will provide you with more information than you could imagine. Dr. Zack Bush's four-minute workout and Tabata four-minute workouts for beginners can be found online. So instead of getting into a long and complicated discussion on the physiology and science of exercise, I have given you a brief breakdown of what you should focus on when exercising.

Remember that for your three-minute workout routine to be effective, it has to be challenging for you. Be sure to do one of the rhythmic, repetitive exercises at least every other day. In between those days, be sure to do something that challenges your strength, endurance, and coordination. Maintain variety in your routines and never do the same exercise two days in a row, even if you took a day off in between. Keep a journal of your workouts and record how you performed in each exercise. For example, write down that you did ninety-five push-ups in three minutes or that you had to stop only four times during your three-minute jump rope session. Compare your performance to the previous workouts and track your progress. Your objective is to see the numbers improve with each workout.

Exercise Trains You to Handle Stress

If you are absolutely honest, you will admit that most mornings you don't want to get up and exercise, even if it's only for three minutes. In fact, when given the choice between staying in bed—or drinking coffee in front of the TV, or reading the newspaper—and doing a three-minute workout, most of us will always choose the other activities over exercise. So it's not really because of the lack of time that we don't exercise. Not many people in this world are so busy that they can't spare three minutes out of their twenty-four-hour day. Let's face it: This is a matter of laziness. I have used every excuse you can think of. I have heard myself say that I'm not a morning person, or my body can't do anything unless I've had my coffee, or I really need those last three minutes of sleep. I've heard them all and used them all.

Countless times, I have gone to bed saying, "Tomorrow I'm going to jump out of bed at 5:00 a.m. and run downstairs and exercise." Then my alarm goes off, and my natural tendency is to tell myself, "I think I will handle my stress much better today if I sleep a bit longer." But this is not true! You will not feel rested and ready for stress if you sleep a bit longer, because your sleep has already been interrupted. You will, however, feel refreshed and accomplished if you do your workout and take a shower.

Taming your Stress Monkey means that getting out of bed is a priority, because it is matched with something you greatly value. For example, I value my relationship with my sons, and their well-being is a priority to me. Therefore, if one of them woke up at 4:00 a.m.

and called out to me for help, nothing would keep me from getting out of bed to help him. If my health is a core value to me and my workouts are a priority, then getting out of bed at 4:00 a.m. to work out should be just as easy as getting up to check on my son. When your core values come into alignment with your priorities, the stress will become tolerable. Read that last sentence one more time and do your best to internalize it. It is a principle of success relevant to any dimension of life.

The problem is that in the morning, logic fails and emotions prevail. Know that you are ruled by your emotions, and attempting to use logic to motivate your lazy butt out of bed never works.

Here is a scenario to consider. Imagine you are sound asleep at 5:00 a.m., and you are suddenly woken up by the sound of your smoke detector alarm. Then you notice that it's difficult to breathe, because your house is filled with thick black smoke. Will you roll over and go back to sleep? Will you say, "I just need five more minutes of sleep"? Of course not! Because you are ruled by your emotions and the emotion in this scenario is fear, that fear will move you to fly out of bed and rescue your family, and it doesn't care if you slept only three hours that night.

What other emotions do you think would motivate you to start your day with action? Think of something that will get you emotionally charged. Play the *Rocky* theme song through your alarm clock when you wake up. Go ahead and admit it—you love *Rocky*! Join a *Biggest Loser* contest with your coworkers. Competition is a great emotional motivator. You can also just choose to get angry at your current state of affairs and get emotionally disgusted with laziness.

You'll also want to use affirmations throughout the day to stay motivated. Create a mantra that defines who you want to be, and repeat it in your head over and over. Like Muhammad Ali, keep telling yourself, "I am the greatest!" Muhammad Ali was an absolute master at using affirmations to maintain an emotionally charged state that motivated him to train harder than anyone else.

So forget about using logic to convince yourself to exercise. Get emotional about it. Stop being controlled by your body's selfish demands. Instead, take charge of your body and make it help you achieve your goals, dreams, and desires. You don't exist to serve laziness; you exist to live life and accomplish great things. Be strong, be courageous, stand firm, have faith, and move forward with conviction. Do this and nothing will stop you.

CHAPTER 12

Step Six: Nourish Your Body

Sacred cows make the best hamburger.

—Unknown

Your Stress Monkey needs to be trained in all three dimensions of stress, and, to achieve true wellness, all three dimensions (physical, psychological, and biochemical) must be addressed simultaneously. Food falls under the biochemical dimension. This dimension has two components: One is to prevent deficiency, and the other is to avoid toxicity. We have already discussed toxicity, so now let's talk about preventing deficiency.

The best way to prevent nutritional deficiencies is to eat a well-balanced diet. Barbara Johnson, the American literary critic, once said, "A balanced diet is a cookie in each hand."[1] I'm sure you enjoyed reading that, but I was talking about a different type of balance. I was referring to a balance between carbohydrates, proteins, and fats. I believe every diet requires all three of these macronutrients.

Nutrition and Supplements

Remember Dr. Terry Wahls's nutrition plan? It is a great example of a balanced diet. Yet if you're like me, you're thinking, *There's no way I can eat nine cups of those vegetables, plus all the other grass-fed meats, organ meats, seaweed, and so on every single day*. If I had MS or another type of autoimmune disease like Dr. Wahls, I would do it, but since, thankfully, that incentive doesn't exist for me, I would rather follow a fairly decent meal plan and use supplements to fill in the blanks.

By definition, supplements are meant to be supplemental to a good diet. The first question to answer is this: Are they necessary? According to an article by the Harvard School of Public Health, "Multivitamins can play an important role when nutritional requirements are not met through diet alone."[2]

It is a proven fact that proper nutrition can help in preventing many fatal diseases, such as cancer and heart disease. It is also a proven scientific fact that proper nutrition is partially responsible for optimum health, superior athletic performance, and ideal brain function. Ideal brain function means mental clarity, great memory, ability to focus, and improved problem-solving abilities.

The Mayo Clinic states that nutritional needs should be met primarily through a diet that is balanced and includes sufficient fruits and vegetables. "For some people, however, supplements may be a useful way to get nutrients they might otherwise be lacking," writes the Mayo Clinic staff.[3]

So Harvard School of Public Health and the Mayo Clinic, as well as most other health authorities, agree nutritional supplements are beneficial. The difference is that some believe you can obtain everything you need in a balanced diet, while others believe it is impossible to constantly and consistently maintain a healthy, nutritious diet in today's fast-paced culture without supplementation. I tend to agree with the latter. I wouldn't say that it is impossible to obtain all your necessary nutrients from food sources. It just requires a great deal of work and diligence.

One reason I recommend supplements is the depleted soils in our farmlands. In previous centuries, farmland had to be "rested" every few years so that it could be replenished with the proper minerals. Unfortunately, this is not practiced in most farms in America today. Some organic farmers do practice crop rotating to protect the soil from mineral depletion. However, it isn't common practice on all organic farms.

I travel abroad quite often, and I've noticed that fruits and vegetables in third-world countries taste so much better than where I live in the United States. I believe the reason for this is that they practice the more primitive farming techniques, and their soils remain rich in nutrients and minerals. Of course, I have also noticed that their produce doesn't look as "perfect" and beautiful as ours here in America, and their produce seems to rot much faster than ours. So it doesn't look as good, but it sure tastes amazing. I still remember the very first time I walked through a grocery store in America. I could not believe how fresh and healthy the produce looked. All the tomatoes were unblemished and perfectly shaped. It sounds funny, but I had never seen anything like it before.

Another reason I recommend supplements is that most produce in grocery stores has such a long transit time. They are typically shipped to your town from as far away as Hawaii, South America, or Southeast Asia. You're probably thinking, *I thought you liked fruits and vegetables from third-world countries.* I do like fruits and vegetables from third-world countries but only when they are fresh and harvested at the proper ripeness. Especially when I am right there to eat them. The produce that makes it over to our grocery stores in the West was picked weeks prior to its peak ripeness so that it could be shipped and stocked before spoiling. When I travel to the Middle East, I see that farmers pick only the ripe fruit from the tree, box the fruit, and sell it the same day in their fruit stands. Which fruit do you believe is more nutritious to our bodies? The one that was allowed to stay connected to its roots until fully ripe or the one that was plucked early and allowed to ripen while sitting on a shelf or in a box?

Finally, the third reason I take supplements daily and highly recommend them is that I am much too busy to invest the time and energy every day into finding and preparing foods that contain all my daily nutrition needs. Most people today don't have the ability to devote so much time and energy to making sure their every meal contains all the vitamins and minerals their body requires.

Then there's the matter of skipped meals. For the record, I am a proponent of intermittent fasting and believe there are health benefits to cycling through a ketogenic nutrition plan from time to time. Also, there are times when we should intentionally not eat to allow the gastrointestinal tract to rest and repair. However, for the purpose of this chapter, which is to discuss preventing nutritional deficiency, I am not going to talk about fasting. Most people I know are skipping meals for all the wrong reasons. They are too busy to sit down and eat three square meals a day, let alone ensure the nutritional balance of those meals. In today's world, very few working people take time to prepare and eat breakfast. Instead, they grab a donut in the breakroom and keep a jar of candy on their desk. Lunch is usually purchased from a fast-food restaurant or deli, and dinner comes premade in a micro-wavable box. Need I say more?

As with my other recommendations in this chapter, the purpose of taking supplements is to increase your body's adaptability to stress and reduce the possibility of a negative response to stress. In other words, your supplements will help strengthen you so you can live and enjoy the life that you want.

So the question to answer next is this: What type of supplements should we take? The polls show that over half of Americans take supplements daily. That number has dramatically increased over the past several decades.[4] However, the health of Americans has not improved over that period. In fact, Americans are now sicker than ever before. Does that mean supplements don't work? Or does it mean that without supplements we would all be a lot worse? The answer is that most of the supplements people are taking simply don't do what they are meant to do—they don't work.

Most of the supplements on the market today are synthetic, meaning they were made from chemicals that resemble their natural counterpart. Since these vitamins and nutrients are artificial, they are not recognized as food by the body. Therefore, their bioavailability and absorbability are limited. The purpose of this segment of the book is not to get into the technicalities and the biochemistry of synthetic vitamins. My objective is to make one simple recommendation. If you want your supplements to work for you, make sure they are whole-food supplements, not synthetic.

You can immediately tell the difference by reading the label. A typical synthetic multivitamin will contain ingredients such as ascorbic acid, cholecalciferol, d-alpha-tocopherol succinate, pyridoxine HCL, and so on. You get the idea. Whereas here is a small list of ingredients you will see on the label of a whole-food multivitamin: carrots, parsley, kale, beets, cabbage, and so on.

Be aware that some vitamin brands claim to be natural and organic. They even have foods listed on the label as the source of their ingredients. However, these vitamins are not whole-food vitamins. They are in fact fractionated vitamins. This is because some experts believe that only a fraction of the whole food is the beneficial part. For example, they believe that ascorbic acid is the only beneficial part of vitamin C and tocopherols are the only beneficial part of the vitamin E complex. Based on that belief, they take only a fraction of the whole and package it into a pill. This allows them to have more of each so-called vitamin in the pill and advertise that their supplements are more potent.

For example, a vitamin C product that contains only ascorbic acid will claim to have 1,000 mg of vitamin C in one pill. The true vitamin C molecule complex is so much larger than ascorbic acid that 1,000 mg would never fit in one pill. In contrast, a whole-food vitamin C pill may contain only 17 mg of true vitamin C, but it is the complete complex formula and not just a fraction of the vitamin. In this instance, the whole-food vitamin C complex might have the following list of ingredients: veal bone, bovine adrenal gland, buckwheat, nutritional yeast, alfalfa, mushroom, defatted wheat germ, echinacea root, carrot, sunflower, and rice bran. Which vitamin C would you rather put in your body? Which do you think will have the most powerful effect? This explains why most people are not getting the health benefits they want from their vitamin supplement. This also explains why there is such a great divide between scientists who believe in the power of vitamins and those who are adamantly against it.

In 2012, an article in *The American Journal of Physiology-Endocrinology and Metabolism* stated that antioxidant supplementation in athletes was "worse than useless." This was based on a research study that revealed "a complete lack of any positive effect of antioxidant supplementation on physiological and biochemical outcomes . . . in human and animal studies."[5]

I agree with their assessment 100 percent. Antioxidants that are made by plants are only for the benefit of plants. Oxygen is toxic to plants, just as carbon dioxide is toxic to humans. You see, plants use photosynthesis to convert light energy to chemical energy. During this process they create and release oxygen, which is a toxic byproduct of photosynthesis. The antioxidants found in plants are specifically designed to protect them from oxygen. Humans, on the other hand, require oxygen to live, and we create carbon dioxide as the toxic byproduct of our metabolism. This is why human cells have their own set of antioxidants, which include superoxide dismutase, catalase, glutathione peroxidase, and others.

Research shows that fractionated antioxidants taken from plants will not only have zero benefit to humans but also inhibit the body's ability to destroy precancerous and cancer cells. The title of one such article, published in *The Journal of Nutrition*, is "Antioxidants Suppress Apoptosis." Apoptosis is also known as cell suicide. Every cell in our body has a predetermined lifespan. When the lifespan is reached, the cell dies. This is part of the body's protective mechanism that kills cancer cells. The article states that "by inhibiting apoptosis, these same antioxidants may exert a cancer-promoting effect in cancer patients and in individuals with precancerous DNA changes."[6] On the other hand, the antioxidants that are naturally present in human cells not only aid in the destruction of cancer cells but also are an important part of the immune system that destroys pathogens (bacteria, viruses, or other microorganisms that can cause disease).

Antioxidants are not vitamins. They are simply protectors of phytonutrients in plants. If a type of plant has high levels of antioxidants, it means that specific plant also has a high level of phytonutrients, and phytonutrients are what we as humans need to be healthy and prevent disease. No wonder so many people are confused about vitamins and antioxidants. They are the same people who persistently take these fractionated vitamins hoping and believing that they are doing a good thing, while they're actually suppressing their immune system and promoting cancer in their bodies. The supplements you take absolutely must be whole-food supplements.

"It is far cheaper in the end to buy the higher priced wholesome foods than to pay the doctor and dentist for services after the damage is done."[7] That statement was made by Dr. Royal Lee, who is also known as the father of natural vitamins. He created the first raw-food vitamin in 1929. In a lecture discussing vitamin E, he stated, "The tocopherols are antioxidants which protect the whole organic complex, but the active principle in the E complex is not the tocopherol, it's the hormone precursors that are found in the green leaf and in the wheat germ oil." In the same lecture he shared the results of a study in which natural wheat germ oil was given to a group of professors at the University of Illinois who were sixty-five years old or older. The result was that the subjects were able to increase their physical endurance by "several hundred percent." He stated that those who were able to ride an exercise bike for only fifteen minutes in the beginning of the study now could ride for two hours after only a "few weeks on wheat germ oil."[8]

Compare the results of Dr. Royal Lee at the University of Illinois with the findings of the scientists in the previously mentioned article that stated that antioxidant supplementation in exercise was "worse than useless." On the surface, it looks as if the two studies contradict each other, but, in fact, they both say the same thing. Antioxidants alone will not benefit us as humans, because they are merely a fraction of the food that nourishes the body. The complete vitamin complex is required to receive the benefit. If your supplement bottle refers to vitamin E as alpha tocopherol, stop taking it. If it says vitamin E in the form of natural wheat germ oil or anything natural with a name you recognize, keep taking it. To take it one step further, you may want to purchase your supplements from manufacturers that grow their ingredients on their own certified organic farms so they can control the quality of their ingredients.

How to Eat

When it comes to taming your Stress Monkey, eating the right foods and taking the proper supplements are, unfortunately, not enough. There is one more aspect to nourishing your Stress Monkey that perhaps will have the biggest impact on your ability to adapt to stress. I am referring to the concept of "how to eat" versus "what to eat." To explain this, let's begin by discussing the relationship between stress and food and where some of our food cravings come from.

We know that our Stress Monkeys love to eat—so much so that we typically overeat. In fact, when we are overstimulated for an extended period of time, we start to crave food. Initially, the cravings will be for sweets and fast-burning carbohydrates, such as candy and chocolate. Over time, if our bodies have been in the fight-or-flight for months or even years, our cravings will begin to include salty foods, such as potato chips and pretzels. When the Stress Monkey is stimulated, the hormone cortisol will be released into the bloodstream. Cortisol will cause increased glucose (sugar) levels in the blood. It also mobilizes triglycerides (fat) into the blood. Triglycerides and glucose are great sources of fuel for our cells. At first, the body will tap into its own sources of sugar and fat, but, very quickly, through the influence of the Stress Monkey, the body decides to conserve its reserves and seek out external sources of sugar and fat. That is why when you are upset, worried, scared, or angry over a long period of time, you begin to crave sugary and fatty foods, such as donuts and ice cream. That's why we call these foods comfort foods.

Statistically speaking and purely based on general research, women are more likely to succumb to overeating and food addictions, whereas men tend to turn to alcohol, smoking, and drugs for comfort.[9] This does not mean that men will not overeat during times of long-term stress. It also does not mean that women are immune from addictions to smoking, drugs, and alcohol as a result of their inability to handle stress.

If your body is not fully equipped to handle the stress in your life, and your Stress Monkey is running wild, these food cravings will most likely win, and you will begin to gain weight. Then, over time, you will begin to experience fatigue. You will wake up in the mornings and won't feel rested. Your energy levels will fluctuate throughout the day, and you will ride the up-and-down energy roller coaster. You will experience brain fog throughout the day. Then when cravings for salty foods become overwhelming, you will also notice that coffee no longer gives you the big boost of energy it used to. In fact, you will find that you can drink coffee in the evening, after dinner, and still be able to fall asleep.

This is a very dangerous place to be. In this stage, you are also experiencing lightheadedness, meaning that when you stand up too quickly, you get lightheaded. This is because your body is not producing the right amount of adrenaline to prevent a blood pressure drop when you get up quickly. Depression is also common during this stage of stress overload. At this point, your blood sugar and triglyceride levels are most likely through the roof, and your doctor may be telling you that you are prediabetic. Your doctor is also probably recommending cholesterol-reducing drugs and telling you that you must lose weight. Eventually, this path leads to full-blown type 2 diabetes, osteoporosis, and even autoimmune disorders. The longer this continues, the harder it is to turn it around. That is why you must properly nourish your body using the best nutrients and supplements.

Some of you may already be experiencing the symptoms I describe in the preceding paragraph. You have extreme food cravings, weight gain, low energy, mental fog, lightheadedness, and depression, and your doctor wants to put you on cholesterol and diabetes medication. If that's you, here's what you need to do: You must stop giving sugar to your Stress Monkey. That includes high-fructose corn syrup. It's not going to be easy, but your life depends on it.

You also must stop consuming artificial sweeteners, and don't eat carb-heavy foods. It's important to not consume caffeine after 3:00 p.m. Instead, increase your consumption of fatty fish such as wild salmon, free-range chicken, grass-fed beef, avocados, and lots of fresh vegetables. Supplement with fish oil, whole-food vitamin D, whole-food vitamin C, and whole-food vitamin B complex, and include coconut oil and olive oil in your diet. Go for a brisk walk for thirty minutes every day, and weight train for twenty minutes three times per week. Sleep longer, and take a ten-minute nap in the middle of the day. When adopting this regimen, please follow your medical doctor's advice, and do it with the intention of naturally reducing the need for medication over time.

Another major cause of the above symptoms is fatty liver. According to Harvard Medical School, "Virtually unknown before 1980, nonalcoholic fatty liver disease now affects up to 30% of adults in the United States and other developed countries."[10] The cause of this epidemic is the large amount of sugar in our diet, especially sugar in the form of high-fructose corn syrup found in soda and other sugary foods. "Today we're even seeing 12-year-old boys with fatty livers because they guzzled soda for years and now need liver transplants," stated Dr. Mark Hyman, a family physician, a four-time *New York*

Times best-selling author, and an international leader in the fields of diabetes and heart disease.[11]

In October of 2006, the American Academy of Pediatrics reported that as much as 13 percent of children have fatty liver, and that number was much higher, 17.3 percent, in teenagers between fifteen and nineteen years of age.[12] Refined sugar causes your liver to increase production of fat. This fat gets deposited around the liver and other internal organs and is called visceral fat. This condition will suppress the liver's ability to produce energy and leads to fatigue and lethargic behavior, even in children. This is also why high-fructose corn syrup has been linked to an increased risk of obesity, diabetes, heart disease, and cancer.[13]

Here are some of the common foods that may contain high-fructose corn syrup: soda, candy, sweetened yogurt, certain salad dressings, coffee creamer, TV dinners, frozen pizzas, canned fruit, fruit juice, certain granola bars, cereal bars, energy bars, energy drinks, breakfast cereals, and ice cream.[14] These are the exact foods that your Stress Monkey will crave during prolonged stressful times.

Keep in mind that this book is not about dieting or how to lose weight. There are plenty of great books on that subject. This book is about taming your Stress Monkey to be able to safely handle any amount of stress without any detriment to your health and well-being. When it comes to this specific subject, the experts will tell you that what you eat is of utmost importance. I completely disagree! The reality is that a lot of people with stress-induced illness actually eat very healthy foods, and they're still getting crushed under the load of the stress in their life. In fact, many of them are adding unnecessary stress to their lives by always worrying about what they're eating.

The secret is that how you eat is much more important than what you eat. For example, citizens of France eat cheese, bread, and wine with practically every meal. Yet they seem to be completely immune to heart disease and obesity. Their healthy bodies are not a result of *what* they eat. They're healthy because of *how* they eat. They relax and eat slowly. They socialize while they eat, and they take great pleasure in consuming every meal.

Do you enjoy your every meal? Do you sit down to eat, or do you grab breakfast and lunch on the go? I know people who eat all the right foods; however, at least one of their meals each day is eaten in the car while driving in heavy traffic. Not only that, but they're yelling at their business associates on their hands-free mobile phone while driving, eating, and checking their email. This person's body is in fight-or-flight mode and is in no physiological condition to be able to digest food. The "healthy" sandwich he's eating will sit in his stomach and turn into a disgusting, fermented mess that his body will have to work overtime to get rid of.

On the other hand, what if you sit down with a friend in a comfortable and pleasant environment, play some soft music, enjoy a good conversation, chew your food slowly, and savor every bite? That food will get digested rapidly and properly. Even if the food isn't the healthiest, your body will pull out every molecule of nutrition and use it as energy and material to build, repair, and regenerate organs, glands, and tissues in your body. You will feel great mentally, physically, and emotionally. To top it off, you reduce your chances of obesity and heart disease, and your Stress Monkey will remain calm, peaceful, and pleasant the whole time.

CHAPTER 13

Step Seven: Listen

This world we live in is the dance of
the creator. Dancers come and go in the
twinkling of an eye, but the dance lives on.

—Michael Jackson, quoted in Harry Eiss,
The Mythology of Dance

M usic is one of the most powerful tools in managing stress. It has a direct effect on the human physiology and psyche. You can completely change or enhance the body's chemistry through music. Music can give you energy when you are tired or bring you joy when you are depressed. It can help you calm down when you are anxious, and it can get you excited when you are not feeling very motivated. The amazing part is that music can neutralize and deactivate a wild Stress Monkey within minutes, sometimes even in seconds. Often the first note of your favorite song can send you into a positive state of mind. It can remind you of your favorite childhood memories or your greatest romantic moments. So turn up the volume, and whenever possible, dance.

Music and Aunt Simi

In 1980, when I was only six years old, I was informed that one of our relatives had just been diagnosed with cancer. Back in 1980, cancer wasn't as prevalent as it is today. It was so rare that when the word "cancer" was spoken, everyone would take a dramatic deep breath, get wide-eyed, and remain silent for a moment. In this instance, the person diagnosed with cancer was one of my dad's cousins, who was one of my favorite people. She used to bring me great gifts and play with me as if she were my age.

I remember when my dad told me that Aunt Simi had just been diagnosed with cancer, she had only six weeks to live, and she was on her way over to our house. Normally, when I would hear that Aunt Simi was on her way over, I would get excited and start jumping around the way a child does on Christmas morning. However, this time I was scared and didn't know how I should act around her. I thought I would have to be mournful around her and not act happy. I thought I should probably try and cry in front of her to show her how sad I was, and maybe that would make her feel better.

Then, Aunt Simi walked in. She was a heavy-set woman with medium-to-short light brown hair. She always dressed well and wore a lot of makeup, as if she were going to a party, and this time was no different. She smiled and laughed the way she always had in the past and greeted me with a big hug and kiss, the way she always did. Then she walked over to our stereo set by the living room wall. It was one of those old, large stereo systems that had a record player on top, a dual cassette player in the middle, and a huge black AM/FM radio receiver underneath. The whole thing sat on top of a display case that encased our family's records and audio cassette tapes. On either side of this monster were two giant speakers that were taller than I was. Aunt Simi walked over, knelt down, and selected a tape out of the display case. Then she stood up, put the tape in the player, pushed Play, and turned up the volume.

The speakers came to life with a song that we all knew very well. It was a famous dance song, and as soon as the beautiful music started, Aunt Simi began to dance. She danced beautifully. She reached out to me and pulled me toward the middle of the living room, and I started to dance with her. We danced so hard that I almost forgot the terrible news. Then she pulled my dad into the middle of the living room, followed by my mom. We were all dancing and laughing until the song ended. Then as we were all still standing together in the middle of our living room, Aunt Simi said, "If I only have six more weeks with you, I'm going to dance and celebrate every single day."

She did exactly that. Throughout her grueling cancer treatments, she listened to music and danced every single day until the very end. The music must have helped her, because she stayed very positive the whole time. She also kept the whole family positive throughout her treatment. Even when her body seemed too weak to stand, she got up and danced. Then, all of a sudden, she started to feel better and stronger. Six weeks became six months and then even longer. She did finally die of cancer, but not for another ten years! Those must have been the best ten years of her life, because a part of each and every day was a celebration, a party.

I believe the music is what kept her alive. Her Stress Monkey didn't stand a chance! The music helped her body to heal. The music kept our family strong. Music can do the same for you. Do what Aunt Simi did. Turn up the volume and play your favorite song.

Once a day for only a few minutes, listen and let the music penetrate your soul. And whenever possible, get up and dance. Every day should be a celebration, and just a few minutes a day can radically improve your life.[1]

Music Is Healing

Think for a moment about the most wonderful time of your life. Was it a family vacation when you were young? Was it when you first fell in love with your spouse? Was it a time when you accomplished something amazing, such as winning the big game, crossing the finish line, or graduating with honors? Was it the day you got married, or was it when you held your child for the first time? What song was playing at that time? Which songs were most popular on the radio back then? Is there a song that can send you back to "then and there" instantly? That's the music you should be listening to every day. That song will act as a tranquilizer to your Stress Monkey, as though you had just shot it with a tranquilizer gun. You will suddenly melt into a calm and relaxed state of mind.

The Chemistry of Music

One of the reasons music has so much power over your Stress Monkey is because it can lead to the release of the neurotransmitter dopamine. Dopamine is a hormone-like substance that helps transmit messages throughout the nervous system. It gets released when we fall in love. It also gets released when we eat chocolate, partake in pleasurable activities, and take mood-enhancing drugs. If something has a feel-good effect in the body, it's because dopamine has been released. Experts say that the reason people get addicted to cocaine is because it causes a surge of dopamine in the body.

On the other hand, a deficiency of dopamine will cause a lack of motivation, fatigue, and depression. Excessive caffeine, alcohol, sugar, recreational drugs, and mood-altering medication will cause dopamine insufficiency. Most of these substances will initially cause an increase in dopamine, which makes you feel good, but, over time, they lead to a deficiency of dopamine. Also, long-term stress in a person whose Stress Monkey is poorly trained will lead to dopamine depletion. This is because the adrenal glands make dopamine, and in long-term situations of stress overload, the adrenals become fatigued and can no longer function optimally to produce dopamine.

Research from McGill University proves that music can cause dopamine to be released in your body.[2] It will make you feel great and combat the effects of negative emotional stress. Music activates the auditory centers of the brain and the centers of the brain that are involved in memory, emotion, motor control, imagery, attention, and abstract thinking. This is why certain music can make you more creative, while other music can help you concentrate, and another type of music can make you a better, faster, stronger athlete. In fact, music can distract your brain from feeling the effects of fatigue. This is why workout music can make you stronger and enable you to train longer before getting tired.

Have you ever noticed what happens to people on the dance floor when their favorite music comes on? Depending on the nature of the party and how much alcohol has been consumed, people seem to go crazy. Usually, when certain songs play, people scream, then throw their arms in the air, jump up and down a few times, and begin dancing as though they don't care if anyone is watching. In September of 2021, *Rolling Stone* magazine released its list of the "500 Greatest Songs of All Time," and at the top of the list was Aretha Franklin's

"Respect."[3] Think about your personal list of the greatest songs of all time, and remember the emotions and energy that those songs evoke in you.

There are also movie soundtracks that can create powerful, positive emotions. For me, some of those movie soundtracks are those for *Rocky*, *Dirty Dancing*, *St. Saint Elmo's Fire*, *The Breakfast Club*, *Titanic*, *The Bodyguard*, and *Saturday Night Fever*. Songs that you love will have a powerfully positive effect on your Stress Monkey. Select a song that moves you in a big way, and listen to it once a day. That's what Aunt Simi did, and it added ten glorious years to her life. Imagine what it can do for you.

CHAPTER 14

Step Eight: Exhale

There is one way of breathing that is shameful
and constricted. Then there's another way;
a breath of love that takes you all the way to infinity.

—Attributed to Jalaluddin Rumi

I am assuming that since you are reading this book, you already
know how to breathe. However, many people don't know there is
a right way and a wrong way to breathe. Furthermore, breathing
serves more functions than just the transfusion of oxygen into the
body. Breathing can serve to detoxify the body. It can relax tense muscles during stressful times and be a tool to help you enter meditative
or hypnotic states. It can be very therapeutic in treating insomnia,
and, most importantly, breathing techniques can be used to set and
regulate the body's neurological biorhythms.

In my years of clinical practice, I have met many people who simply did not know how to breathe properly. There are two parts to proper breathing. One is the actual mechanics of breathing, which involves the muscles you are using and how you are using them. The second is the rhythm of your breath and the relative ratio of time between inhaling and exhaling.

Let's start with the mechanical part of breathing. The main muscle used in breathing is the diaphragm. This muscle sits horizontally at the base of your rib cage. When you breathe in, the diaphragm contracts. It moves down and expands the lungs and creates a vacuum that pulls air into the lungs. When you exhale, the diaphragm relaxes, moves back up to compress the lungs, and pushes the air out of the lungs.

Professional singers are masters at using their diaphragm to control the amount of air leaving their lungs, thus enabling them to sustain musical notes and control sound volume properly. Becoming more conscious of the diaphragm is also essential when using breathing techniques to increase your ability to adapt to stress.

Most people naturally use the diaphragm to breathe when they are relaxed. However, during strenuous exercise we need more help to get the oxygen that the body needs, and this causes us to engage auxiliary muscles. These muscles are located around the neck and rib cage. So when you are relaxed and breathing properly, the only muscle that should be working is the diaphragm. When you are working hard and your body needs more oxygen, such as when lifting weights, riding your bike, or running, the neck and rib cage muscles contract to help the diaphragm pull more air into the lungs, and then the abdominal muscles contract to forcefully push the air back out of the lungs. All of this works in unison to provide for your body's oxygen needs, depending on your body's demands for air.

What does all of this have to do with stress? Well, when you are in a state of high stress, as in a state of fight-or-flight, your breathing pattern changes. Let's look at a real-life example.

The Earthquake

In 2011, I was having a business meeting in my office, sitting with a couple of bank executives. Our meeting was almost over when suddenly it seemed my desk started to move up and down in front of me, and so did the chairs we were sitting in. The windows began to rattle, and we heard creaking sounds from the structure of the building. The whole thing continued for a few seconds, and then everything stopped. Our eyes were wide open, our hearts were racing, and we were all breathing faster than before. We had just experienced an earthquake in Maryland, where earthquakes are extremely rare.

Even though none of us in that meeting were performing strenuous exercise, all of us were using our auxiliary muscles to breathe. Our physiology was in a state of fight-or-flight. But within another minute, when we all realized we were safe, our breathing pattern returned to normal. The auxiliary breathing muscles relaxed, and the diaphragm continued to do its job of pumping air in and out of our lungs. If we had stayed in a state of negative stress longer than just a few minutes, our neck and shoulder muscles would have developed tension and would have begun to feel stiff. If we had stayed in that state for several days, we would have developed increasing discomfort and pain in the neck, and the stiffness would have further limited the range of motion of the neck and shoulders, and eventually we could have suffered tension headaches. This is why so many people with untrained Stress Monkeys get tension headaches. You can avoid all of this by paying attention to your breathing pattern.

The Rhythm of Breathing

There is one other problem that occurs during times of perceived negative stress. As mentioned previously, the rhythm of our breathing is important to our health. First, everything in the body has a rhythm, and the different rhythms of the body coordinate with each other through the nervous system to keep our body at optimum function and performance. Brain waves have a rhythm, the heartbeat has a rhythm, the cerebrospinal fluid that circulates around the brain and spinal cord has a specific rhythm, and even the peristalsis with which our digestive tract works has its own rhythm.

Another reason that your breathing pattern has to have a rhythm is because the lungs need time to allow for the exchange of oxygen and carbon dioxide in our blood. The blood that passes through our lungs needs time to expel the carbon dioxide and become saturated with oxygen. That means, to allow for this process to take place, air must remain stagnant in the lungs for a period of time before it is exhaled. The time requirement for inhaling versus exhaling needs to be a one-to-two ratio, meaning it should take you twice as long to exhale as it takes to inhale. For example, if it takes two seconds to inhale, it should take four seconds to exhale.

This rhythm is essential for proper oxygen saturation during rest or times of minimal physical exertion, such as sitting here typing on a computer. This rhythm becomes distorted when we experience perceived negative stress. The ratio between time to inhale and time to exhale becomes one to one; meaning if it takes you two seconds to inhale, your time to exhale will also equal two seconds. During times of severe negative stress, you may even find yourself holding your breath.

Most people don't have the skill or the ability to accurately control the rhythm and rate of their heart, cerebrospinal fluid circulation, blood pressure, or intestinal tract. However, we can all very easily control our breathing rate and rhythm, and the good news is that by consciously controlling our breathing, we ultimately positively affect all other biorhythms.

Breathing Exercises

You need only two simple exercises to help you properly handle stress and reduce the possibility of a negative outcome from stress. First, let's work on training your body to breathe using only the diaphragm and none of the auxiliary muscles. To do this, lie down flat on your back with your knees bent. Place one hand on your chest and the other hand on your abdomen. Breathe naturally and just observe the pattern in which your chest and your abdomen move with each breath.

Some people will notice that their chest rises every time they inhale, and others will notice that their abdomen rises every time they inhale. Which one do you think is the healthy way to breathe when resting? That's exactly right: If you are breathing with your diaphragm, the abdomen is the only body part that should move when breathing. If your chest is rising on inhalation, you are using your auxiliary muscles, and you may be setting yourself up for a negative stress response with ensuing health problems.

Before we discuss any stress-relieving exercises, you must make sure your body learns to properly breathe, using the diaphragm. Here is your assignment. Beginning today, you must spend sixty seconds per day practicing diaphragmatic breathing. So, for sixty seconds, lie down on the floor and place one hand on your chest and the other on your abdomen. Then just breathe without allowing your chest to rise. Do this for the entire sixty seconds. Once this becomes easy for you and you can do it without much concentration, do the exercise sitting at your desk or standing in line at the post office. Within one month, this should become the new normal breathing pattern for you. Once this happens, you may move on to the more advanced exercises, which I describe next.

I mentioned that during times of stress our breathing rhythm is altered. You can battle the negative stress response by spending just a few minutes per day doing a simple breathing exercise. The exercise requires you to take just ten deep breaths once or twice per day. During this exercise, you must stay focused on your breathing and count in your mind how long it takes you to slowly take a deep breath. You can also use the help of a stopwatch, but this will become impractical and unnecessary as you quickly become more skilled at this exercise.

Sit somewhere comfortable to do this exercise. I don't recommend lying down to do this, because you may fall asleep. While seated comfortably, begin to inhale as you count in your mind up to five. Inhale as deeply as you can and use your auxiliary muscles to fully fill your lungs with air. Then begin to exhale slowly for a count of ten—twice as long as it took you to inhale. You can count as fast or as slow as you like as long as you keep the same pace throughout the exercise. Initially you may find that it is actually difficult to exhale slowly. This is an indication that you have been in a state of fight-or-flight for too long. If you exhale through your mouth, it becomes easier to control the rate at which air exits your lungs. Take ten deep breaths twice per day, and you will notice a major improvement in the level of stress and tension that you feel on a daily basis.

When you first begin to practice this breathing exercise, you may get lightheaded or begin to hyperventilate. If this happens, immediately stop doing the exercise for that day, begin again the next day, and continue until you can do all ten breaths without difficulty.

A final word of caution: Do not ever do this exercise while driving. It can make you sleepy or lightheaded, and those are very dangerous states to be in when driving.

The benefits of this exercise go a long way in improving the body's adaptability to stress. For example, this exercise may help people who suffer from acute insomnia. There may be times when you are under so much stress that you cannot shut down your mind to go to sleep at night. I have experienced this in the past when the same thoughts circulated around and around in my head, and I just couldn't fall asleep. It is a very frustrating feeling, especially when you keep looking at the clock and calculating how many hours of sleep you've lost and how important it is that you fall asleep and get a few hours of rest before your busy day tomorrow.

If you ever face such a situation, just start taking really slow, deep breaths, and follow the preceding instructions to maintain a one-to-two ratio between your time to inhale and time to exhale. This will reset your neurological biorhythm, and you will most likely not make it to your tenth breath before you fall into a deep sleep. The important part is to make sure you breathe very deeply, as slowly as you can, and maintain the rhythm of exhaling twice as long as it takes you to inhale.

There is another very valuable benefit to deep breathing that I want to discuss with you. In addition to restoring the natural rhythms of the body and helping you fall asleep at night, this breathing exercise will serve to cleanse and detoxify your body. It does this by improving lymph flow through the lymphatic system. The lymphatic vessels of the body are commonly referred to as the body's sewer system. The following is an overly simplified illustration of a very complex system. Similar to the sewer system that keeps our city streets clean by removing rainwater and waste, the lymph channels keep the blood clean by removing metabolic waste, transporting white blood cells, and excreting cancer cells.

Given this description, you can imagine that the flow of lymph is extremely important to our health and well-being. The critical part in all of this is that the lymphatic vessels are not connected to a pump that would keep the lymph flowing through the body. There are only three ways by which the lymph system circulates and cleans the body. One is by physical exercise. Muscle contraction creates the pumping action that pushes the lymph through the vessels. Massage is the second method of lymph transport through the body. In addition to helping reduce muscle stress, massage can significantly boost the immune system by promoting lymph drainage. The third and final way of promoting lymph drainage is by taking deep breaths. Deep inspiration creates the vacuum and subsequent pressure required to pump the lymph through the channels. The more lymph we pump through our system, the more toxins we will remove from the body, and the healthier we will be.

Furthermore, researchers have discovered that one of the reasons dieting alone does not produce the weight-loss results that we expect and hope for is that the body is unable to rid itself of toxins.[1] As a protective mechanism, the body will store toxins in adipose (fat) tissue. If the body does not hide the toxins in fat cells, the toxins can circulate throughout the body and make us ill. Therefore, the more toxins in the body, the more reluctant the body will be to shed the fat. The result is the frustration that people experience when dieting does not produce the desired effect of weight loss. I have seen many of my patients begin to lose weight simply by breathing properly and doing this breathing exercise twice daily. A body that has fewer toxins is much more capable of handling and adapting to stress.

While we are on the subject of weight loss, see if you can answer this question: Where does fat go when it is lost? Have you ever wondered about that? It doesn't just disappear, so it has to go somewhere. Theory number one is that it becomes energy and gets used by the body. Another theory states that it gets excreted from the body through sweat, urine, and feces. Some people believe that fat is actually converted to muscle when we exercise.

As you may have guessed, all these theories are incorrect. Burning fat does create energy, but that's not how the actual fat leaves the body. The chemical makeup of all organic (meaning living) material is based on the element carbon. Body fat is no different. The chemical formula of a molecule of body fat (the most common being triglycerides) is $C_{55}H_{104}O_6$. That means there are fifty-five carbon atoms in every molecule of fat. Since carbon is much larger than hydrogen, fat is composed of mostly carbon. When we breathe in, we take oxygen from the air. What comes out when we exhale? That's right, carbon dioxide. Oxygen (O_2) goes in, and carbon dioxide (CO_2) comes out. The most efficient way to lose fat is to exhale it.[2]

This is yet another reason for you to do the suggested breathing exercise. It regulates your biorhythms, detoxifies your body, gets rid of fat, and teaches your Stress Monkey to safely handle stress without causing neck pain and tension headaches. Who could ask for anything more?

CHAPTER 15

Step Nine: Sleep

When thou liest down, thou shalt not be afraid:
Yea thou shalt lie down, and thy sleep shall be sweet.

—Proverbs 3:24

Why do so many of you deprive yourselves of sleep? The answer is obvious and the same reason you skip meals and miss your workouts. Everyone is too busy to sleep. You know exactly what sleep deprivation feels like, and I am sure you don't like it. Sleep is when the body repairs itself and the brain detoxifies. A tremendous amount of metabolic, physiological, and psychological work takes place when you sleep. In a blog post on sleep and longevity, Dr. Oz stated that "the deepest and most regenerative sleep occurs between 10:00 p.m. and 2:00 a.m. After 2:00 a.m., your sleep becomes more superficial."[1] Therefore, going to bed early may be much more effective in combating sleep deprivation than sleeping in late. Yet it seems that most of us do it in reverse. We try to catch up on sleep by staying in bed longer rather than by going to bed early. Sleep deprivation will not only lead to physical fatigue but also cause a host of psychological and emotional problems, including impaired judgment, difficulty concentrating, depression, aggression, and impulsive behavior. Some researchers go as far as stating that sleep deprivation can be responsible for criminal activity and violence.[2] I am not sure how accurate that is, and I certainly don't think that a few sleepless nights will turn you into a criminal. However, the detrimental effects are very real and must be taken extremely seriously.

Poliquin Group, founded by the world-famous strength coach and author Charles Poliquin, recommends that we pick a regular bedtime and follow it even on weekends. This allows you to take advantage of your natural circadian rhythm, optimize your body temperature, and release the proper hormones, such as melatonin and leptin, when you sleep. As a result, you will have more energy, burn more fat, and sleep better. In an article titled "Practical Ways to Get Better Sleep," Poliquin Group writes, "Studies show people with trouble sleeping tend to improve when they have a set bedtime that is between 9:30 and 11:00 p.m."[3]

I agree with the concept of going to bed at the same time every night and waking up at the same time every day. Experts claim that the body needs between seven and nine hours of uninterrupted sleep per night. This range was determined by measuring the levels of different hormones in the body as they respond to sleep. This can quickly become very complicated, especially when you take into account the different types of sleep, such as light non-REM (rapid eye movement) sleep, deep slow-wave sleep, and REM sleep, and how each results in a different hormonal response.

Here is what you need to know: The deeper your sleep and the more time you spend in deep slow-wave REM sleep, the healthier your brain and body will be. If you don't get enough deep sleep, your cortisol levels will increase and your growth hormone levels will decline. Over time, increased cortisol levels will lead to metabolic problems such as increased body fat, osteoporosis, and insulin resistance. Insulin resistance is the precursor to type 2 diabetes. In fact, the American Diabetes Association has announced that poor sleep is a leading cause of type 2 diabetes.[4] Increased cortisol levels are also linked to mental problems, such as memory loss, which become more severe with age, indicating that our amount of quality sleep seems to decline with age.[5] Declining levels of growth hormone are linked to reduced muscle mass, decreased strength, increased body fat, suppressed immunity to infectious diseases, and overall decline in health. In summary, inadequate sleep is one of the biggest contributors of aging.[6]

The Circadian Rhythm

Life has a rhythm. Biologists refer to this as the circadian rhythm. It is a twenty-four-hour internal clock that runs automatically and can adjust and adapt to the environment based on daylight. The more rhythmic your daily routine of sleep, the healthier and more adaptable to stress your body will become. In other words, the stricter you are with your sleep schedule, the better your Stress Monkey will serve you in handling life stress. Disruptions in the circadian rhythm are greatly detrimental to your health. This is most evident in people who sleep at odd times during the day. In fact, in 2007, the World Health Organization warned that people who work at night and sleep during the day have a higher risk of developing heart disease and cancer. So much so that they classified night shift work as a probable carcinogen.[7]

The natural hormone melatonin is responsible for regulating your circadian clock. Melatonin is released when we sleep in the absence of light. Daylight prevents the production of melatonin. This is especially significant for people who work at night and sleep during the day. Since light blocks the production of melatonin, those of you who do shift work and sleep at odd times must absolutely make certain that you sleep in pitch-black darkness. That means you need to cover the windows with blackout curtains. Also, those of you who sleep with a night-light should consider turning it off when you sleep. You should cover up the alarm clock and block the light that it emits as well. And if you happen to wake up in the middle of the night to use the bathroom, do your best not to turn on any lights, and refrain from checking your cell phone. Any light that hits your eyes will stop melatonin production and prevent you from getting the most out of your sleep for the rest of the night.

A deficiency in melatonin will cause sleep disorders. This creates a vicious cycle, leading to lower melatonin levels. This leads to worse sleep, which further lowers melatonin levels in the body. Research shows that declining levels of melatonin increase the risk of developing degenerative diseases of the brain, such as Parkinson's and Alzheimer's. It may appear that supplementation with melatonin would be a good idea, but I advise caution, just as I do earlier in this book when I discuss vitamin D. You must consult with your health-care professional before taking oral melatonin, because it may adversely react with other conditions or medications.

In the same way that the best type of vitamin D is what your body produces when your skin is exposed to natural sunlight, the best type of melatonin is the type your body produces when asleep in darkness. If you do choose to try supplementing with melatonin, keep your dose between 0.5 mg and 3 mg. If you experience drowsiness the next day or if you get a headache, reduce your dose. Melatonin taken in higher than 5 mg doses can cause the opposite effect and actually keep you awake, or it may cause you to not be able to sleep the next night.

One of the world's foremost experts on sleep physiology is Dr. Matthew Walker. He is a neuroscientist who has dedicated his career to studying sleep and the health ramifications of improper sleep. In 2017 he published the groundbreaking book *Why We Sleep: Unlocking the Power of Sleep and Dreams*.[8] Dr. Walker states that, despite popular belief, supplementing with melatonin does not really help you get better sleep, but it does help you if you are traveling and your circadian rhythm does not match the time zone you are in. Taking melatonin can trick your body into believing it is dark outside. Based on this, melatonin may be a useful supplement for those who need to sleep during the day and those who travel frequently.

Dr. Walker further cautions that there is another reason those who travel a lot will not be able to sleep properly. He states that half your brain will not sleep when you are in a hotel room or in an environment that isn't your home. This is your body's threat-detection mechanism that prevents deep sleep anytime you are in an unfamiliar environment. In such instances, even if your melatonin levels are normal, your body and brain still fail to replenish themselves during sleep.

Staying on the subject of melatonin, you should know that there are foods that naturally contain melatonin. These include bananas, oats, rice, ginger, barley, tomatoes, radishes, and red wine. From a dietary standpoint, you can also consume foods that contain tryptophan. It is an amino acid that is used by the body to produce serotonin, and serotonin is then converted to melatonin. So another natural way to increase melatonin is by eating foods rich in tryptophan. These include milk, yogurt, cottage cheese, nuts, chocolate, oats, seafood, turkey, chicken, beans, rice, eggs, pumpkin seeds, and sunflower seeds.

Based on these lists, I bet one thought is running through your head: All I need is chocolate, cheese, and red wine to have great sleep! I caution you not to take this information out of context. Keep your dietary choices consistent with everything else we have been talking about. I am not against eating chocolate, cheese, and red wine. Just don't overdo it, and don't drink wine every night. Also, remember my advice about supplements. Foods and whole-food supplements that contain natural B vitamins (especially B-6 and folate), zinc, magnesium, and omega-3 fatty acids will also aid in the production of melatonin.

Sally's Story

Several years ago, a patient of mine told me that his wife, Sally, had been admitted to the hospital following attempted suicide. Sally and her family were long-term patients of mine and visited my office routinely for wellness checkups. They had a very stable and loving marriage with two small children in private school. From her husband's perspective, their life was perfect, and he could not figure out why his wife of over twelve years would have tried to kill herself.

Sally was a detective with the police department in a neighboring city. She was a decorated officer, and her career had been full of commendations, awards, and promotions. After she was diagnosed with severe clinical depression, I went to the hospital to visit her.

At first, she was too emotional and embarrassed to discuss her condition with me, but, as we began to discuss her lifestyle, it quickly became apparent why she was clinically depressed. It turns out that she worked the night shift during weeknights. She would get home as the kids were getting up to go to school. After helping the kids get ready and dropping them off at school, she would go home and sleep until it was time to pick them up from school. She would then stay awake the rest of the day doing house chores and spending time with her children until they went to bed, and she would then go back to work as a police officer.

In their master bedroom, directly over their bed, was a large skylight. When building their home, they had placed it there because they wanted to be able to gaze at the stars at night. However, when she slept, from morning to the early afternoon, the sun shone brightly through that window directly on her face. Now, imagine the stress of dealing with criminals every night and risking your life for the sake of protecting the public. Then add to that stress the deficiency of melatonin because of exposure to light during sleep. Further add the increased cortisol production of not enough deep sleep and the decline in growth hormone for the same reasons. This is the perfect storm and an explosive recipe for disaster.

Sally said that recently she'd felt as if she was getting sick more often. She had noticed that she was gaining weight from uncontrollable food cravings. She had also begun to experience forgetfulness, mood swings, and extreme irritability. These are classic signs of sleep deprivation and insulin resistance caused by high cortisol fluctuations. It is no wonder she was so depressed. I quickly made several recommendations, but the most effective of my recommendations was for her to begin sleeping in a different room during the day.

She started to sleep in the guest room and was able to seal the windows with heavy blackout curtains so that no light could enter the room when she was sleeping. Within thirty days, her serotonin and melatonin levels returned to normal, and she was herself again.

Today, Sally and her husband are still happily married, raising their children in a loving and stable environment, and our detective is fully equipped to handle the stress of her job without detriment to her health. Her Stress Monkey is working for her, not against her.

The moral of the story is that proper sleep is not just necessary for physical health. It is also critical for psychological health and emotional stability.

Sleep Quantity and Quality

Dr. Walker, the "Sleep Diplomat," claims that proper sleep requires quantity and quality, and it is impossible to compensate for one with the other. Meaning, if the quality of your sleep is poor, you cannot make up for it by sleeping longer. Likewise, if you're not sleeping enough, having really deep high-quality sleep will not reduce your chances of ill health. Dr. Walker adamantly states that shorter sleep equates to a shorter lifespan. He further states that sleep is not a renewable resource, meaning that if you lose an hour of sleep tonight, you cannot make up for it the following night, because the damage has been done.[9] A study conducted by researchers at the University of Michigan's Frankel Cardiovascular Center saw a 24 percent increase in the number of heart attacks on the Monday following daylight saving time every spring. They reported that most heart attacks seem to occur on Mondays, and on this particular Monday every year, when we get one less hour of sleep, 24 percent more people have heart attacks than any other Monday. Just as shocking is the fact that there is a 21 percent decrease in the number of heart attacks after returning to standard time in the fall, when we regain our lost hour of sleep.[10]

In another study reported by Dr. Walker, a group of healthy adults who slept six hours per night for one week were compared to healthy adults who slept eight hours per night. According to Dr. Walker, over seven hundred gene expressions were distorted in the group that slept six hours per night. Half of the distorted genes genetically increased the activity of cells that cause tumor growth, long-term chronic inflammation, and cardiovascular disease. The other half of the genes that were distorted caused the decline in immune function.[11] This means that those who slept six hours per night for a week activated genes that cause disease and deactivated the genes that prevent disease and fight infections. In a similar study, those who slept for four hours displayed signs of immune deficiency and an increased risk of developing cancerous tumors. They also displayed a 72 percent decrease in anticancer immune cells called natural killer cells that target and kill malignant cells. This occurred after just one night of sleeping only four hours.[12] The results should be quite sobering for those of you who brag about being able to function on inadequate sleep.

If that's not enough encouragement to increase your time asleep, take a look at the alarming results of another study published in the journal *Sleep* in 2003. "Chronic restriction of sleep to 6 hours or less per night produced cognitive performance deficits equivalent to up to 2 nights of total sleep deprivation," reported the authors.[13] The study basically revealed that if you sleep six hours per night for ten days in a row, your mental function and ability will be equivalent to someone who hasn't slept at all for two consecutive nights.

The only difference was that the group that didn't sleep at all for two nights admitted their mental deficits and stated that they were too sleepy to function. The group that slept six hours per night were completely unaware that their neurocognitive behavior had declined so dramatically. When asked to self-report, they sincerely believed they were fine on only six hours of sleep per night. Meanwhile, when scientifically assessed, they showed a decline in their ability to reason, access short-term and long-term memory, pay attention or maintain focus, and learn new things. The authors of the study further stated that "sleep deprivation has a neurobiological 'cost' which accumulates over time."[14] This reinforces the statement by Dr. Matthew Walker that sleep is not a renewable resource. Every single sleepless night has long-term ramifications that accumulate over time. If you want your Stress Monkey to be trainable, you must sleep a minimum of seven (quality) hours per night.

In addition to sleeping seven hours per night, one of the best methods of taming a sleep-deprived Stress Monkey is by taking daily ten-minute naps. Research shows that naps improve your mood and counteract some of the symptoms of sleep deprivation. According to the American Academy of Sleep Medicine and WebMD, the most effective naps are only ten minutes. Those who take a ten-minute nap tend to experience less sleepiness and fatigue throughout the day. They also have better mental and cognitive performance. Napping for a longer period of time can actually backfire. Those who nap for thirty minutes or longer tend to experience drowsiness and feel sleepier upon waking from their nap.[15]

Usually when I recommend the ten-minute nap, my patient's first response is that ten minutes isn't even long enough to fall asleep. The good news is that you don't actually have to fall asleep. You just need to rest for ten minutes. Lie down or recline in a chair, set your alarm for ten minutes, and close your eyes. It's as simple as that. In fact, the reason you are groggy after longer naps is because your brain was allowed to go into a deeper sleep cycle, and you interrupted the cycle by waking up. The benefits are much more if you never go deep into a sleep cycle. Have you ever been awakened from a nap and for a minute you didn't know where you were or what time of day it was? That happens when your sleep gets interrupted in the middle of a deep sleep cycle, and that's how you know your nap was too long. When you interrupt a deep sleep cycle, you also cause an increase in cortisol. This is the exact outcome we're trying to avoid. If you limit your naps to ten minutes, you are in no danger of going too deep.

There is some data that shows a ten-minute nap between 2:00 p.m. and 4:00 p.m. will cause an increase in growth hormone.[16]

Growth hormone helps you maintain your muscle mass, repair injured tissues, burn body fat, protect your bone density, and keep you looking young. I believe one reason the afternoon nap is affectionately referred to as a beauty rest is because it causes a spike in growth hormone. In general, napping will result in a better mood, less sleepiness, more energy, improved heart function, lower blood pressure, and less anxiety.

Dr. Walker also recommends the afternoon nap. His studies of brain waves show that there is a decrease in brain wave activity in the afternoon as a normal part of our circadian rhythm. According to Dr. Walker, the reason we get sleepy after lunch isn't always related to what we had for lunch. It's because our biological systems just naturally slow down a little bit in the afternoon. This is yet another good reason to take a short nap.[17]

Sometimes your Stress Monkey just refuses to go to bed. He refuses to rest and keeps you from being able to sleep. We refer to this as insomnia. There are many different causes of insomnia. The main one is the inability to properly handle stress. Whenever the amount of stress on the body exceeds the body's ability to safely adapt, your Stress Monkey begins to act out, and one of the outcomes is insomnia. This is when you find yourself saying, "I'm too tired to fall asleep." I refer to this state as wired-and-tired. You lie down to sleep and your thoughts take over, running through your mind in a circular pattern, keeping you from being able to relax your mind. This is because you are in the state of fight-or-flight, also known as sympathetic overdrive. Your Stress Monkey is behaving as if you are being chased by a pack of hungry wolves and doesn't want you to fall asleep, because if you do, you'll be eaten by the wolves. If insomnia is a concern of yours, reread the chapter on breathing and begin doing the breathing exercise whenever you lie down to sleep.

Many people take prescription and over-the-counter medication to help them fall asleep. Studies of brain wave activity reveal a disheartening fact that sleep aid drugs block REM sleep, and, as discussed earlier, the most beneficial part of sleep is REM sleep, in which the brain has dreams.[18] This is another reason I don't recommend drinking alcohol at night to help you sleep. We know that alcohol blocks dream sleep, because alcoholics who undergo withdrawal experience extreme hallucinations. Medical experts believe these hallucinations are the brain's attempt to catch up on all the dreaming the person missed out on when they were drinking. My recommendation is to try every natural remedy before resorting to chemical sleep aids.

Have you ever noticed that you sleep better when you're at the beach? I've heard many people say they get their best sleep when vacationing near a beach. Do you know why? There are two reasons for this phenomenon, and they're not what you might think. One is called grounding or earthing. The beach is one place where everyone loves to walk barefoot. Walking barefoot allows you to absorb free electrons and minerals from the ground.[19] It literally grounds you. When grounded, we are able to fall asleep much faster and easier.

I learned about this concept from Dr. Jeff Spencer. He is the doctor for the US Tour de France teams. At a conference, he revealed a few of his secrets on how his athletes were able to perform at such high levels and recover so quickly from injuries. According to Dr. Spencer, the good news is that you don't need to travel to the nearest beach whenever battling insomnia. Just go outside and walk barefoot on the grass or the ground for about ten to twenty minutes. You will find that you can return to bed and fall fast and deep into Lalaland.[20]

The second reason you tend to sleep better when by the beach is the ionizing effect that the ocean waves have on the air you breathe. As the waves interact with air molecules, they create negatively charged ions in the air. Breathing this air has a cleansing effect on your body. Experts say air that is high in negative ions can enhance mood, suppress allergic reactions, reduce headaches, and improve the function of your immune system.[21] Wherever there is pollution-free fresh air, you will find more ions, but the highest concentrations of ions are near moving water such as waterfalls, rivers, and ocean waves. Pure fresh air that is packed full of negatively charged ions will calm your Stress Monkey and help you get more benefit from your sleep.

If you don't live next to a waterfall and the ocean is not within daily driving distance of your home, then unfortunately this information helps you only when you're on vacation. You do get exposed to ionized air every time you take a shower because of the running water. You can also install a waterfall or a fountain in your home. There are quite a few air ionizers on the market, and many air purifiers have built-in ionizing technology; however, not enough research has been done on these devices, so I don't feel comfortable recommending them. Your best bet is to spend some time in nature breathing fresh air on a regular basis.

Sleep plays a crucial role in your ability to adapt to stress. First and foremost, do your very best to get at least seven hours of sleep at night. If you must sleep during the day, make sure you sleep in pitch-black darkness. Stay consistent with your schedule of when you go to sleep and when you wake each day. Take a ten-minute nap daily in the afternoon. Do not ingest any caffeine within six hours before going to sleep. To prepare for bedtime, turn off half the lights in the house a few hours before going to bed. This will trigger melatonin release and prepare your body for a restful and deep sleep. Also cool the house down by a few degrees before going to bed. Dr. Walker says cooler temperatures will enable you to fall asleep faster and go deeper into REM sleep. You can also take a hot bath before bed. The heat around your body will cause a decrease in your core temperature, and you will be able to sleep deeper and better.[22]

These are easy and simple recommendations, but their impact on your health will be monumental. Soon your friends and relatives will be asking you how it is that you are able to stay so young and vibrant.

CHAPTER 16

Step Ten:
Start a Movement

A revolution is coming — a revolution which will be
peaceful if we are wise enough; compassionate if we care
enough; successful if we are fortunate enough — but a
revolution which is coming whether we will it or not. We
can affect its character; we cannot alter its inevitability.

— Robert F. Kennedy, speech to the US Senate,
May 9, 1966

Revolution

When I was five years old, I remember sitting in the back seat of my
family's blue Datsun. For those of you who don't remember, Datsun
was a brand of car that was owned by the Nissan Motor Company.

My dad was driving, my mom was sitting in the front passenger seat, and we were headed to my friend's house for his sixth birthday party. I was so excited. All my friends from kindergarten were going to be there.

Dad was maneuvering through the typical Tehran traffic, and we were making good time, until we turned the corner on the street and suddenly came to a complete stop. Protesters were in the street, and they had completely blocked traffic. The military police on the other side of the street were wearing riot gear. This didn't look good.

All of a sudden, batons were drawn, tear gas was thrown at the protesters, and fighting broke out. It was as though we were on the set of a movie, and the director had just yelled, "Action!" Mom and Dad quickly ordered me to get down on the floor of the car, and I did. I could hear yelling and screaming from outside the car. Mom and Dad would also utter comments like "Oh, my gosh" and "Oh, no!" A couple of times something or someone hit our car, and the whole car shook.

I was probably too young to realize the full gravity of the situation, because I wasn't scared. I was just curious. I kept thinking about those action/adventure movies that I loved to watch so much. It was the most exciting thing for me to be in the middle of all that action, and I really wanted to look out and see what was going on, so I did. I slowly lifted my head up from the floor of the car and peeked over the edge of the car door. The first thing I saw was a man in a white button-up shirt, gray pants, and black leather shoes walking diagonally toward the rear of our car. He wasn't really walking; he was stumbling. There was a lot of bright red blood on his shirt. He had a full beard, and his face showed agony and pain. His arms were outstretched toward the sky as if he were praying. I could hear his voice, but I couldn't tell what he was saying. At first, I thought I was imagining things, but as he took another step closer, I realized what I saw was real. He had a large butcher knife stuck in his chest. He took another step forward and fell to his knees. He then started to fall forward, but before his chest hit the ground, I ducked back down to the floor of the car and never looked out again.

I remember that scene today as if it were just yesterday. That was the start of the Iranian revolution in 1979. It was violent and bloody. Many people lost their lives for what they believed in. They fought because they believed their country would be better for it.

I do not discuss the political ramifications of the Iranian revolution. Nor do I discuss my personal beliefs about the situation and circumstances that followed. The reason I share this experience with you is to give you a glimpse into what a revolution looks like. However, not all revolutions need to be violent in nature.

The United States has also had its share of revolutions. As a nation, we have faced many challenges. The Declaration of Independence sparked a revolution and marked the beginning of our free nation. What would have happened if the people of that time had stood on the sidelines and watched?

The Civil War was a revolution. It was a war for freedom for all people, and the result was the abolition of slavery. What if people had sat around and done nothing?

The Great Depression led to a revolution that produced a new economy and led to prosperity. Those who took action made a difference. What if no one had taken action?

The civil rights movement was a revolution and a fight for equal rights for all races. What if Rosa Parks had moved to the back of the bus? What if Dr. Martin Luther King Jr. had kept his great dream to himself?

America's New Challenge: Sickness

Today, America is facing a new challenge: sickness. We are in a health crisis, and it is killing our people, destroying our families, and crushing our economy. To overcome this crisis, we need a new revolution.

Are we a healthy nation? Look at the numbers. In a report titled "National Health Expenditures and Selected Economic Indicators," which was produced by the Centers for Medicare and Medicaid Services in 2019, the cost of health care was expected to reach $4 trillion in 2020 and is projected to grow to $6.2 trillion in 2028.[1]

If we are a healthy nation, then why is the cost of health care expected to explode by over 60 percent in ten years?

Just to put things in perspective, $5.7 trillion can pay for 230 million mid-size sedan cars. That would mean a brand-new car for almost everyone who has a driver's license in America, each and every year.

In spite of all the money being spent, life expectancy is declining. "Doctors Warned Life Expectancy Could Go Down, and It Did" was the title of an article posted on the *Smithsonian* website on September 21, 2012.[2] On December 9, 2010, WebMD reported that US life expectancy has declined by a tenth of a year and that this is the third time in the past thirty years that life expectancy has decreased.[3]

The reason life expectancy is dropping isn't because the elderly are dying. It's because more children and young people are losing the battle against chronic lifestyle diseases. We need a revolution.

Our children are sicker than ever before, suffering from what were formerly considered adult diseases. Why are teenagers suffering from type 2 diabetes, heart disease, and arthritis? We have made so many advances in medical technology, yet we seem to be going backward in health. This is not okay. It is not acceptable. We need a revolution.

In the 1980s, experts announced that dietary fat is the reason for heart disease and obesity. You may remember the incredible fat-free rice cake! Following that item, every food company began to produce their own fat-free versions of their products. Thus began the fat-free revolution. What happened to our health? The occurrence of obesity soared into record highs. According to the CDC, "During 1980–2008, obesity rates doubled for adults and tripled for children."[4] Perhaps we shouldn't have eliminated dietary fat.

In the 1990s, we decided that sugar was the culprit. We always believed that eating a lot of sugar and simple carbohydrates could cause diabetes, but in the 1990s we learned that high levels of sugar in the diet also leads to obesity and heart disease. And because of the removal of fat from our diet in the 1980s, more people were eating high levels of "fat-free" carbohydrates. That was why the rates of obesity and heart disease were growing. So all food companies jumped on the bandwagon and began to produce sugar-free products.

Thus, the sugar-free revolution was born. So what happened to our health? The occurrence of diabetes soared into record highs. According to the CDC, "The number of new cases of diabetes changed little from 1980 through 1990 but began increasing in 1992. From 1990 through 2010, the annual number of new cases of diagnosed diabetes almost tripled."[5] That is the exact opposite of the outcome they intended. Not only did it fail to reduce the prevalence of obesity; the introduction of artificial sweeteners, diet drinks, and zero-calorie foods resulted in a threefold increase in the number of people suffering from diabetes. Perhaps sugar-free wasn't the answer either.

Stress as the New Culprit

Today it seems that Americans are revolting against stress and calling it the number one cause of disease in America. After decades of adding processed "fat-free" and "sugar-free" foods to the diet, falsely believing that modified food produced in a factory is superior to nature, we are seeing that our health is significantly worse than ever. Now the so-called experts have turned away from blaming fat and sugar and are focusing on fighting a new foe called "stress" as the new culprit for poor health.

"Stress doesn't only make us feel awful emotionally, it can also exacerbate just about any health condition you can think of," says Jay Winner, MD, author of *Take the Stress out of Your Life* and director of the Stress Management Program for Sansum Clinic in Santa Barbara, California.[6]

So many health-care trendsetters of today want you to take the stress out of your life. Would you like to know what a stress-free country looks like? It's a country full of couch potatoes. It's a country with high unemployment rates and zero entrepreneurs. It's a country that produces nothing and in which new inventions are nonexistent. That is not what this beautiful nation was created to be by our ancestors.

All great endeavors come with a degree of stress. Anything worth doing is stressful. Pursuing higher education has stress. Starting a family comes with stress. Building a new business is full of stress. Chasing your dream will be stressful. Living a "stress-free" life means you won't do any of those things.

But this is America, the land of opportunity and the place where dreams come true. Going "stress-free" will be the death of that. It will have the same effect that going "fat-free" and "sugar-free" had on our bodies, so don't let it happen. Tell everyone you know that stress is not the problem. The inability to handle stress is the problem. How great our nation becomes depends on how much stress we as citizens can handle.

Will You Help Lead the Revolution?

So who do you think should solve this problem? The government's efforts to make drugs and surgery more accessible will help the sick, but it will not answer the question of why so many of our citizens are so deathly ill. The pharmaceutical companies are producing medication that can help only after disease has overtaken the body. The result is more drugs that mask symptoms without any effort toward the prevention of disease. The insurance companies have a financial obligation to their stakeholders to protect profits, and the only way to do so is by denying necessary services and reducing the doctor's reimbursements. As a result, doctors are required to see more patients in less time to earn the same amount of income. A good number of doctors are choosing not to participate with insurance companies anymore. Those medical professionals, who proclaim the benefits of early detection, are concerned only about catching diseases earlier and intervening faster. Their efforts are not contributing anything toward prevention and elimination of the cause of disease. The whole system is a house of cards, and it's about to collapse on us.

On the other hand, the chiropractic profession is focused on improving the function of the body to make people more resilient against disease. In a discussion post on www.mercola.com, Dr. Mercola made the following statement: "Additionally, researchers have also found that chiropractic adjustments affect the chemistry of biological processes on a cellular level! And that chiropractic care can affect the basic physiological processes that influence oxidative stress and DNA repair. So there's a whole lot more to chiropractic care than just whipping bones into place."[7]

Dr. Mercola was referring to the famous serum thiol study that stated that patients under long-term chiropractic care demonstrated significantly higher thiol levels in their blood. Serum thiol is used by the cells of the body to protect and repair our DNA, thereby reducing the effects of aging and preventing cancer.[8] By that fact alone, chiropractic care should be a staple in every person's lifestyle.

On November 26, 2000, the *Chicago Tribune* published an article titled "New Respect Boosts Chiropractic as a Mainstream Therapy." Staff writer Connie Lauerman reported on an HMO insurance company that uses chiropractors as primary care physicians in Illinois. According to the article, replacing the medical doctor with chiropractors as the general practitioners resulted in an almost 80 percent reduction in hospitalization, an almost 85 percent reduction in outpatient surgery, and a 56 percent drop in pharmaceutical drug usage.[9]

These are not small numbers. Statistically, even a 10 percent reduction in hospitalization, outpatient surgery, and pharmaceutical drug usage would be an astounding savings for the federal budget. What would the economy look like if the cost of health care were cut by half? This is not just a money issue. The dollars spent are representative of sick and suffering people. So if hospitalizations are reduced, that means fewer people in hospitals, fewer people disabled, fewer people in nursing homes, and certainly fewer grieving family members.

In the article "Medicare Folly," Dr. Christopher Kent discusses the results of a study that surveyed 311 chiropractic patients aged sixty-five years or older. The chiropractic patients were compared with US citizens of "similar health status" and age. The results revealed that "the chiropractic patients spent only 31% of the national average for health care services." He further reported that "the chiropractic patients also experienced 50% fewer medical provider visits compared with US citizens of the same age." In other words, when chiropractic care was properly utilized, people spent nearly 70 percent less money on health care and needed 50 percent fewer doctor visits.[10]

There's no question about it: We need a revolution.

In his inaugural address in 1961, President John F. Kennedy said, "Now the trumpet summons us again—not as a call to bear arms, though arms we need—not as a call to battle, though embattled we are—but a call to bear the burden of a long twilight struggle, year in and year out, 'rejoicing in hope; patient in tribulation,' a struggle against the common enemies of man: tyranny, poverty, disease, and war itself. . . . Will you join in that historic effort?"[11]

Today, in the same way, I ask you to join me in this effort and step up to this new challenge. We don't need government officials to solve this one. All revolutions begin with only a handful of people, a group of like-minded friends who decide to do things differently and to live life according to their values and beliefs. Let's be the revolution!

All mass movements and social shifts have occurred because a small group of rebels stood up for what they believed was right. Historically, those people would have been ridiculed or, worse yet, persecuted, and if that becomes our fate for being healthy, then so be it.

Let's begin by taming our Stress Monkeys. Let's take charge of our health. Let's reclaim our lives. Then, let's set an example for our children and grandchildren and those who look up to us. Let's get our friends and coworkers involved and build small groups of people who don't shy away from stress. These groups will focus on improving their adaptability to stress, becoming powerfully healthy and successful in the process. These small groups can lead to revolutionary communities of ultrahealthy people. They will be communities of people who value God, family, health, and service to others. They will understand the power of innate intelligence and will implement the ten steps of taming their Stress Monkeys. Starting this peaceful revolution is as simple as that.

Be the revolution!

I have a vision: The United States of America will someday be deemed the wellness capital of the world. I still think this is the greatest country on the planet. It has been my home for the past three decades. I'm proud to be a citizen of the land of the free, the home of the brave, the defender of democracy, the protector of life, liberty, and the pursuit of happiness for all people. "The first wealth is health," said one of America's greatest advocates of social reform, Ralph Waldo Emerson.[12] If prosperity cannot exist in a society of unhealthy people, then life, liberty, and the pursuit of happiness for all must include health.

The time is now. It is up to you and me. Will you be a part of the revolution? Will you join this movement and turn your biggest stress into your greatest strength?

My hope is that this book has provided you with a new perspective on wellness that will become the foundation on which you build your life. It is also my vision that future generations will look to you as an example and a role model of how to care for themselves and their family members.

Let's get started.

The Practice of Chiropractic Care

One should first get a knowledge of the structure of the
spine; for this is also requisite for many diseases.

—Hippocrates, "On Joints"

What Is Chiropractic Care?

"You get your back cracked and you feel better" is what the woman
sitting next to me on the airplane said when I asked her what she
knew about chiropractic care. She followed that statement by saying,
"Thank goodness I've never needed to see a chiropractor; I've never
had back pain."

Chiropractic care was discovered in 1895 by Daniel David Palmer.
He believed that spinal alignment directly affects the function of the

nerves, the spinal cord, and the brain. He built the chiropractic profession on the basis that an abnormality in the spine will interfere with the health of the individual.

Over the past century there have been many published research articles and case studies that support Dr. Palmer's claims. There are also many experts and specialists who dispute his claims, stating that spinal misalignments cannot affect the function of the spinal cord and cannot interfere with nerve impulse conduction.

The fact is, chiropractic care is the second-largest field in health care and the largest of the alternative-to-medicine professions. Incidentally, it is also one of the youngest fields in health care. It is newer than acupuncture, homeopathy, naturopathy, osteopathy, and Ayurvedic medicine. Why is it that one of the youngest fields in health care has quickly become the most popular and successful among alternatives to mainstream medicine? Would it have grown so much and so fast if it wasn't effective? Would it have so much support and such a strong following if it didn't work?

Since its inception in 1895, chiropractic has passed the test of time. It has been on trial and was upheld by the Supreme Court of the United States in *Wilk v. American Medical Association*. The literature supports its effectiveness to the point that the United States Government, the Veterans Administration, Medicare, and all major insurance companies will cover and reimburse chiropractic services.

So what is chiropractic care?

Chiropractic is the method by which the health of the spine is analyzed and enhanced. The spine protects the spinal cord and supports your body weight. That alone is enough reason to make spinal health a priority.

Consider the profession of dentistry. It is the method by which the health of your teeth is analyzed and enhanced. The teeth serve to help with digestion and primarily are used to bite, tear, and chew food. Dentists claim that if teeth are not properly maintained, the result will be tooth decay and gum disease. They further claim that if misalignments in teeth are not corrected using braces, they can result in problems with biting, chewing, and speaking, as well as headaches and earaches. In fact, most dentists will state that a healthy mouth makes for a healthy body.

I can't think of anyone who would publicly disagree with any of these claims about dentistry. If these claims are true about teeth, then how much more important is it to maintain a healthy spine? If a misalignment of teeth can cause earaches and headaches, how much more can a misaligned spine affect your health?

At a recent business convention, the CEO of a mid-size company told me that he would never go to a chiropractor because "once you have something 'cracked,' you have to keep getting it 'cracked,' and it'll never feel normal again unless you keep cracking it."

That wasn't the first time I'd heard that one. It's rarely spoken by people who have experienced an actual chiropractic adjustment. Typically, people say this because of a past experience that caused them to fear chiropractic adjustment. Or they may be someone who has a habit of cracking their knuckles. As with any habit, they seem to keep doing it and tend to mistakenly believe that adjusting the spine is similar to cracking their knuckles. This couldn't be further from the truth.

Others attempt to adjust their own necks and backs. This is not advisable, because it is impossible to deliver a specific chiropractic adjustment to yourself. You will either fail to correct the specific misalignment, or you will move the spinal joints beyond their normal range of motion. Neither scenario is desirable.

A chiropractic adjustment, by definition, must be specific. For example, through an X-ray analysis, your chiropractor may find that the first bone in your neck, called the atlas (or C1), is tilted to the left or rotated to the left. Your chiropractor would then contact only the bone or vertebra that is misaligned and apply a very specific force in a very specific direction to return only that vertebra, in this case C1, back to its normal and natural position. Once this adjustment takes place, and assuming there are no other subluxations in your spine, you will most likely lose your ability and desire to "pop" your own neck. Also, the health benefits of a specific adjustment are endless. As I explained this to the CEO at the business convention, he asked, "Then why do people have to keep going back to the chiropractor?"

That is a valid question. Most of my patients continue to see me as their chiropractor for many years. They refer their children, siblings, parents, and friends and encourage them to stay under care long term. So I don't blame you if you also believe that once you see a chiropractor, you're stuck having to go for the rest of your life. However, the premise behind this belief is where the confusion arises.

I respectfully explained to the CEO that just by having a chiropractic adjustment, you don't become dependent on getting regular adjustments. That's like saying once you start exercising in a gym, you have to keep going for the rest of your life. Or once you start eating organically grown produce, you have to continue doing it for the rest of your life. Similarly, it's like saying once you see a dentist for a professional dental cleaning, you have to keep going for the rest of your life. Or once you brush your teeth, you have to regularly brush them for the rest of your life. You would laugh if I said that once you have your cholesterol checked, you have to keep getting it checked for the rest of your life. My CEO friend got the point. In fact, at the end of our conversation, he asked if I could recommend a chiropractor in his area.

The fact is that you may choose to see a chiropractor for a specific period of time to correct a spinal problem, or, like most people, you may decide that you would like to maintain proper spinal hygiene by visiting your chiropractor on an ongoing basis. The truth is that you don't have to, but why wouldn't you go to a chiropractor regularly for the rest of your life? It's the perfect way to protect your greatest investment, which is your health. It is also a critical step in taming your Stress Monkey.

To expand on this point, let's continue the comparison between chiropractic and dentistry. What does a dentist most commonly search for when examining your teeth? Cavities! What does a chiropractor search for when examining your spine? Subluxations! The difference is that a subluxation is a whole lot more serious and detrimental than a cavity. A subluxation is a neuro-spinal dysfunction. In other words, it is a problem in the spine that affects the function of the spinal cord and spinal nerves. Nerves are used by the brain to monitor and communicate with all parts of the body, including organs, glands, blood vessels, joints, and muscles. Therefore, a subluxation is anything that interferes with the brain's ability to properly monitor and control the functions of your organs, glands, blood vessels, joints, and muscles.

If you have teeth, you are undeniably susceptible to cavities, and if you have a spine, you are most definitely susceptible to subluxations. What would happen if you decided to ignore a cavity and not get it filled by your dentist? The common belief is that the cavity would rot through the entire tooth, painfully irritating the nerve, and then begin to affect the surrounding teeth. Eventually, it would cause tooth decay and gum disease in the entire mouth.

Comparatively, let's discuss what would happen if you decided to ignore a spinal subluxation and not get an adjustment to correct it. The affected spinal joint would begin to degenerate, become arthritic, and irritate the nerve root. The arthritis would spread to the surrounding vertebral joints and eventually cause arthritis throughout a large region of the spine.

Have you ever gone to a dentist for a routine checkup and been given the bad news that you have a cavity? Why didn't you already know about the cavity? Why did you have to wait until the dentist told you about it? This is because a cavity has no signs or symptoms in its early stages, and by the time the tooth begins to hurt, the cavity is most likely so advanced that the tooth may need a root canal, or, worse, the tooth may need to be extracted.

In the same way, a subluxation by definition is silent or asymptomatic, which means it typically has no signs and symptoms. In fact, by the time a subluxation begins to cause pain, it has already advanced to arthritis—inflamed spinal joints and degeneration. So you don't necessarily have to feel anything to have a cavity, and you certainly don't have to have any pain to have a subluxation in your spine.

If someone has a cavity, can he or she fix the problem by exercising, doing yoga, taking pills, or getting acupuncture? Of course not! All those things are helpful in their own way, but they do not fix or fill a cavity. In the same way, if someone has a misalignment or subluxation in the spine, he or she will not be able to correct the problem by doing yoga, getting a massage, lifting weights, taking vitamins, eating broccoli, taking medications, or getting injections.

Thankfully, there is a safe and effective way to have our subluxations corrected before and after debilitating consequences set in. And that's the amazing and powerful chiropractic adjustment. Just as a cavity can be fixed only by a dentist, an adjustment can be delivered only by a qualified, trained, licensed, and board-certified chiropractor.

So if you don't necessarily feel subluxations, how can you know if you have one? How does a chiropractor determine whether a subluxation is present in your spine? The answer is very similar to how your dentist determines if you have a cavity in your teeth. Your dentist will examine your teeth, but to be certain, he or she will routinely take X-rays to look for cavities. A chiropractor will also take X-rays to measure and analyze the alignment of the vertebral column and determine whether a subluxation exists.

Although X-rays are most valuable in detecting subluxations, they alone are not sufficient to determine the presence of a subluxation. The chiropractor will also look for neurological patterns that may have been functionally affected in your body. This is because, by definition, a subluxation must affect the function of the nervous system. Patterns of neurological dysfunction are determined by the following types of testing: balance and coordination testing, thermal patterns surrounding the spine revealing blood circulation irregularities, and muscle tone analysis at rest and in motion.

If you are like a lot of my patients, your eyes began to glaze over as you read the last sentence. I completely understand that not everyone shares my enthusiasm and passion for the scientific description and explanation of subluxations. Therefore, if you would like, you have my permission to skip to the "Subluxations Simplified" section in this appendix. However, if you are a science geek like me, then buckle your seat belt, because I'm going to take us on a scientific journey to explore the supportive evidence behind subluxation and the efficacy of chiropractic.

Subluxations in Detail

Since a misalignment alone is not enough to confidently conclude that there is a problem, we use these subluxation models to determine whether the nervous system is being affected and to what extent it is damaging your health.[1]

1. *Dyskenesia* (also known as pathomechanics). This refers to abnormal segmental motion in the spinal column. Abnormal motion in a specific segment of the vertebral column will result in ligamentous tugging. Ligaments are tissues that are found

around every joint, and their job is to hold two bones together. Ligaments are strong fibrous tissues that have almost no elasticity, meaning they do not stretch or elongate under tensile stress. This is why a misalignment will result in tugging of the ligaments around the joint. Tugging of the ligaments and abnormal motion of the segment will result in focal inflammation that can be seen on an MRI. This inflammation in the joint when left uncorrected will result in degenerative changes and fluid in the marrow of the bones at the areas where the affected ligaments are attached. This is not visible on an X-ray and will be easily missed unless we use a high-resolution MRI. Finally, when this condition is left alone, it will result in osteophytosis (formation of bone spurs). The bone density must change between 30 percent and 50 percent from normal before the degeneration can be visible on an X-ray. Some experts have said it may take up to fifteen years of degenerative change before a bone spur is large enough and dense enough to be seen on an X-ray. The point here is that a subluxation can go undetected for many years. During that entire time, progressive degeneration is taking place and will eventually result in permanent loss of joint function. Furthermore, the resulting disc protrusion, bone spurs, and ligament hypertrophy (thickening) will cause the spinal canal to narrow, which will ultimately cause spinal cord compression. Not only will this type of degenerative change cause local irritation and pain, but it can also compress the nerve roots that are the major extensions of the spinal cord that branch off to exit the spinal column and connect to the various organs, glands, tissues, and blood vessels. Dyskenesia can be quantified through range of motion analysis using a dual digital inclinometer or motion imaging studies, such as an X-ray, CT, or MRI.

2. *Dysafferentation.* In simple terms, dysafferentation refers to the inaccurate perception of the environment by the nervous system. The nervous system relies on sensory input to properly perceive its environment. For example, the fact that you know the ground under your foot is level is because mechanoreceptors and proprioceptors in the joints of your foot sent that information to your cerebellum (part of your brain). That is called sensory or afferent information. If the ground under your foot was uneven but this information did not reach your cerebellum, you would be susceptible to accidentally spraining your ankle and falling to the ground. Afferent input is how you know whether your environment is warm or cold, dry or wet, loud or quiet, uphill or downhill, light or dark, and so on. Afferent input is also how you can tell whether the person in front of you is a friend or foe, happy or sad, or offended by you or offensive toward you. Dysafferentation is the process by which a subluxation will interfere with the inflow of information to the brain and the nervous system's perception of its surroundings. Just as dyskinesia can cause degeneration and arthritis, dysafferentation can result in poor balance and coordination, as well as inappropriate behavior such as ADHD. If the brain does not receive proper neurological input from the outside environment, it cannot function normally. Dysafferentation is a viable explanation of how a subluxation in the atlanto-occipital junction (C0-C1 joint) of Dr. Kevin's spine was causing his seizures, and why correcting that subluxation allowed for his brain to function normally.

3. *Neurodystrophy.* This refers to the effect of a subluxation on tissues and organs of the body with regard to the endocrine system and the immune system. According to the neurodystrophic

model of subluxation, interference with the nervous system causes stress in the body, resulting in a sympathetic response and a decline in the strength of the immune system. This is the basis of disease progression in the body. As the sympathetic nervous system is altered by a subluxation, the body's response to infectious agents is also altered.

The best way to illustrate this concept is to look at a couple of research studies. One study showed that spinal adjustments in the upper to mid back caused an improved immune response in the subjects. The researchers measured the amount of neutrophils in the blood. Neutrophils are the most abundant type of white blood cells, and they function to rid the body of harmful bacteria, fungi, and other foreign material. The results of the study showed that only fifteen minutes after the adjustment, there was a significant increase in the white blood cell count as compared to blood neutrophil levels before the adjustment.[2]

In a different controlled study, patients who were positive for human immunodeficiency virus (HIV) were used as subjects to study the effect of chiropractic adjustments on the immune system. HIV attacks and destroys CD4 cells. CD4 cells, also known as T-lymphocytes, are a type of white blood cell that plays a major role in protecting your body from infection. They detect viruses and bacteria and then activate the immune system. Patients infected with HIV gradually lose all their CD4 cells and become completely immunocompromised. In this research study, chiropractic adjustment of the upper neck resulted in a 48 percent increase in CD4 cells, while the control group (subjects who did not receive the chiropractic adjustments) experienced a 7.96 percent decrease in CD4 cells.[3]

The research shows the nervous system is directly involved in the control and monitoring of the immune system. Therefore, any interference in the function of the nervous system will directly affect the body's ability to prevent disease and recover from an illness. In other words, a bad connection in your nervous system will render your Stress Monkey weak and powerless. Almost all healing, repair, and regeneration of bodily tissues (that is, muscles, bones, organs, glands, and blood vessels) occur while the body is in the parasympathetic state of the nervous system, and negative stress causes a sympathetic response. Therefore, according to the scientific evidence, sustained and continuous negative stress that is caused by a spinal subluxation will, over time, significantly reduce the body's ability to rest, repair, regenerate, and heal itself. Thus, it is of vital importance to regularly monitor the spine for subluxations and to get adjusted at the first sign of spinal subluxation.

Subluxations Simplified

If you decided to skip the previous section, here's a brief explanation. A subluxation can begin with either a misalignment or immobility (fixation) of a bone in the spine. This will lead to degeneration of the disc and joints at that particular level. As degeneration progresses, discs will bulge, bones will form bone spurs, and the joint capsules will become thicker. The bulging discs, the bone spurs, and the thickening of tissues will take up space and compromise the canal in which the spinal cord rests. The result will be painful spinal joints, eventual compression of nerves that exit the spinal column, and compression of the spinal cord itself. Compression of the spinal cord or the exiting nerve roots will interfere with the brain's ability to monitor and control the organs, glands, blood vessels, muscles, and joints. In addition to pain, the end result will be gradual, progressive decline in organ function and overall health, all of which

could have been avoided if the health of the spine had been monitored and maintained by a chiropractor. Therefore, before you begin
to tame your Stress Monkey, it is of utmost importance to ensure that
the nervous system is devoid of any interference. Your ability to turn
stress into success depends on it.

Notes

Introduction

1. Thomas Edison, "Edison Hails Era of Speed," *Fort Wayne Sentinel*, December 31, 1902, p. 49.

2. World Health Organization, "Widespread Misunderstandings about Chronic Disease—and the Reality," 2005, https://www.who.int/chp/chronic_disease_ report/media/Factsheet2.pdf.

3. Paula W. Yoon, Brigham Bastian, Robert N. Anderson, Janet L. Collins, and Harold W. Jaffe, "Potentially Preventable Deaths from the Five Leading Causes of Death—United States, 2008–2010," *Morbidity and Mortality Weekly Report* 63, no. 17 (2014): 369–374.

4. Centers for Disease Control and Prevention, "Diabetes Report Card 2012," 2012, https://www.cdc.gov/diabetes/pubs/pdf/diabetesreportcard.pdf.

5. Gary Taubes, "What If It's All Been a Big Fat Lie?" *New York Times Magazine*, July 7, 2002, https://www.nytimes.com/2002/07/07/magazine/what-if-it-s-all -been-a-big-fat-lie.html.

6. S. M. Artaud-Wild, S. L. Connor, G. Sexton, and W. E. Connor, "Differences in Coronary Mortality Can Be Explained by Differences in Cholesterol and Saturated Fat Intakes in 40 Countries but Not in France and Finland: A Paradox," *Circulation* 88, no. 6 (1993): 2771–2779; S. Renaud and M. de Lorgeril, "Wine, Alcohol, Platelets, and the French Paradox for Coronary Heart Disease," *The Lancet* 339, no. 8808 (1992): 1523–1526.

7. Robyn Braun, "When Harmless Bacteria Go Bad," *Scientific American*, December 1, 2013, https://www.scientificamerican.com/article/when-harmless -bacteria-go-bad/.

Chapter 1

1. E. J. Raven, "Patrick Gentempo Jr, DC and G. Russell Reiss, MD," *YouTube*, July 30, 2008, https://www.youtube.com/watch?v=WlQLGp8k-6o.

2. Darren Rovell, "Muhammad Ali's 10 Best Quotes," *ESPN*, June 3, 2016, https://www.espn.com/boxing/story/_/id/15930888/muhammad-ali-10-best-quotes.

3. Eric Plasker, *The 100-Year Lifestyle* (Avon, MA: Adams Media, 2007), 5.

4. Plasker, *The 100-Year Lifestyle*, 5.

5. Renee Stepler, "World's Centenarian Population Projected to Grow Eightfold by 2050," Pew Research Center, April 21, 2016, https://www.pewresearch.org/fact-tank/2016/04/21/worlds-centenarian-population-projected-to-grow-eightfold-by-2050/.

6. Desiree Adib, "100 Years Old and Water Skiing," *ABC News*, November 22, 2005, https://abcnews.go.com/GMA/ESPNSports/story?id=1329254.

Chapter 2

1. James L. Chestnut, *The Wellness Prevention Paradigm* (Victoria, BC: TWP Press, 2011).

2. Nancy Cooper, "World's Best Hospitals, 2021," *Newsweek*, September 5, 2021, https://www.newsweek.com/best-hospitals-2021.

3. Chestnut, *The Wellness Prevention Paradigm*.

4. World Health Organization, "World Health Organization Assesses the World's Health Systems," February 7, 2000, https://www.who.int/news/item/07-02-2000-world-health-organization-assesses-the-world's-health-systems.

5. Kathleen Geier, "Shocker Stat of the Day: Life Expectancy Decreases by 4 Years among Poor White People in the U.S.," *Washington Monthly*, September 22, 2012, https://washingtonmonthly.com/2012/09/22/shocker-stat-of-the-day-life-expectancy-decreases-by-4-years-among-poor-white-people-in-the-u-s/.

6. Michael Devitt, "CDC Data Show U.S. Life Expectancy Continues to Decline," American Academy of Family Physicians, December 10, 2018, https://www.aafp.org/news/health-of-the-public/20181210lifeexpectdrop.html.

7. Rich Mendez, "U.S. Life Expectancy Dropped by 1.5 years in 2020, Biggest Drop since WWII," *CNBC*, July 21, 2021, https://www.cnbc.com/2021/07/21/life-expectancy-in-the-us-declined-in-2020-especially-among-people-of-color-.html.

8. Kelli Miller, "How Many Kids Need Cholesterol Drugs?" *WebMD*, February 16, 2009, https://www.webmd.com/cholesterol-management/news/20090223/how-many-kids-need-cholesterol-drugs#1.

9. "Should Children Take Statin Drugs to Lower Their Cholesterol?" *Consumer Reports*, June 2010, https://www.consumerreports.org/cro/2012/05/should-children-take-statin-drugs-to-lower-their-cholesterol/index.htm.

10. Hans Selye, *The Stress of Life*, 2nd ed. (New York: McGraw Hill, 1978).

11. John Ortberg, *Everybody's Normal till You Get to Know Them* (Grand Rapids, MI: Zondervan, 2003).

12. Dan Diamond, "The Ebola Number You Haven't Heard: 80% of U.S. Ebola Patients Have Survived," *Forbes*, October 21, 2014, https://www.forbes.com/sites/dandiamond/2014/10/21/the-ebola-number-you-havent-heard-80-of-u-s-ebola-patients-have-survived.

13. Dream Life Journey, "Dr. Norman Vincent Peale—Positive Thinkers Always Get a Positive Result," *YouTube*, January 24, 2017, https://www.youtube.com/watch?v=EQHI9CV-EdU.

14. Ortberg, *Everybody's Normal*.

15. Selye, *The Stress of Life*, xii.

16. "America's 50 Top Givers," *Forbes*, 2014, https://www.forbes.com/special-report/2013/philanthropy/top-givers.html.

Chapter 3

1. Joan Schiller, "Cancer Q&A: Why Do Some Smokers Never Get Lung Cancer, and Others Who Don't Smoke End Up Getting It?" University of Texas Southwestern Medical Center, 2011.

Chapter 4

1. Nina Isoherranen and Thomas M. Burbacher, "The Use of Nonhuman Primates in Evaluating the Safety of Therapeutic Medications Used during Pregnancy," in *Primate Models of Children's Health and Developmental Disabilities*, ed. Thomas M. Burbacher, Gene P. Sackett, and Kimberly S. Grant (New York: Elsevier, 2008), 325–376.

2. Neil Vargesson, "Thalidomide-Induced Teratogenesis: History and Mechanisms," *Birth Defects Research, Part C: Embryo Today* 105, no. 2 (June 2015): 140–156.

3. Rachel R. Huxley, "Nausea and Vomiting in Early Pregnancy," *Obstetrics and Gynecology* 95, no. 5 (May 2000): 779.

4. Zena Stein and Mervyn Susser, "The Dutch Famine, 1944–1945, and the Reproductive Process, I: Effects on Six Indices at Birth," *Pediatric Research* 9 (1975): 71–72.

5. Bruce H. Lipton, *The Biology of Belief: Unleashing the Power of Consciousness, Matter and Miracles* (Carlsbad, CA: Hay House, 2010).

6. Gina Kolata, "Human Genome, Then and Now," *New York Times*, April 15, 2013, http://www.nytimes.com/2013/04/16/science/the-human-genome-project-then-and-now.html.

7. Lipton, *The Biology of Belief*.

8. Wei Zhang, Lynette Moore, and Ping Ji, "Mouse Models for Cancer Research," *Chinese Journal of Cancer* 30, no. 3 (March 2011): 149–152.

9. Lipton, *The Biology of Belief*.

10. Earl S. Ford, Manuela M. Bergmann, Janine Kröger, Anja Schienkiewitz, Cornelia Weikert, and Heiner Boeing, "Healthy Living Is the Best Revenge: Findings from the European Prospective Investigation into Cancer and Nutrition," *Archives of Internal Medicine* 169, no. 15 (2009): 1355–1362.

11. Dean Ornish, "What's Good for You Is Good for Our Planet," *Time*, November 11, 2014, https://time.com/3579106/eating-meat-vegetarian-global-warming/.

12. Diabetes Prevention Program Research Group, "Reduction in the Incidence of Type 2 Diabetes with Lifestyle Intervention or Metformin," *New England Journal of Medicine* 346 (February 2002): 393–403.

13. Dean Ornish, "What's Good for You Is Good for the Planet," TEDx Talks, November 17, 2012, https://www.youtube.com/watch?v=QYmInK5xo6g.

14. D. Ornish, A. M. Gotto, R. R. Miller, D. Rochelle, and G. Mcallister, "Effects of a Vegetarian Diet and Selected Yoga Techniques in the Treatment of Coronary Heart Disease," *Clinical Research* 27, no. 4 (1979): 720A.

15. Dean Ornish, Gerdi Weidner, William R. Fair, Ruth Marlin, Elaine B. Pettengill, Caren J. Raisin, Stacey Dunn-Emke, et al., "Intensive Lifestyle Changes May Affect the Progression of Prostate Cancer," *Journal of Urology* 174, no. 3 (September 2005): 1065–1069.

16. James L. Chestnut, *The Wellness Prevention Paradigm* (Victoria, BC: TWP Press, 2011).

17. Chestnut, *The Wellness Prevention Paradigm*.

18. James Chestnut, interview by Thomas R. Lamar, *Spinal Column Radio*, episode 166, August 3, 2013.

Chapter 5

1. "5-Foot-3 Woman Lifts Car off Child," *Spokane Daily Chronicle*, December 6, 1979, p. 57.

2. David Gelles, James B. Stewart, Jessica Silver-Greenberg, and Kate Kelly, "Elon Musk Details 'Excruciating' Personal Toll of Tesla Turmoil," *New York Times*, August 16, 2018, https://www.nytimes.com/2018/08/16/business/elon-musk-interview-tesla.html.

3. Jean Ferrières, "The French Paradox: Lessons for Other Countries," *Heart* 90, no. 1 (January 2004): 107–111.

Chapter 7

1. "Passing of Pathognomonic Symptoms," *Journal of the American Medical Association*, August 12, 1905, p. 468.

2. Daniel J. DeNoon, "Chiropractic Cuts Blood Pressure," *WebMD*, March 16, 2007, https://www.webmd.com/hypertension-high-blood-pressure/news/20070316/chiropractic-cuts-blood-pressure#1.

3. Alan J. Forster, Harvey J. Murff, Josh F. Peterson, Tejal K. Gandhi, and David W. Bates, "The Incidence and Severity of Adverse Events Affecting Patients after Discharge from the Hospital," *Annals of Internal Medicine* 138, no. 3 (2003): 161–167.

4. Michael O. Schroeder, "Death by Prescription," *U.S. News and World Report*, September 27, 2016, https://health.usnews.com/health-news/patient-advice/articles/2016-09-27/the-danger-in-taking-prescribed-medications.

5. Schroeder, "Death by Prescription."

6. John Zhang, Douglas Dean, Dennis Nosco, Dennis Strathopulos, and Minas Floros, "Effect of Chiropractic Care on Heart Rate Variability and Pain in a Multisite Clinical Study," *Journal of Manipulative and Physiological Therapeutics* 29, no 4 (May 2006), https://pubmed.ncbi.nlm.nih.gov/16690380.

7. Ogi Ressel, *Kids First: Health with No Interference* (Garden City Park, NY: Square One, 2006), 85.

8. Ressel, *Kids First*, 84.

9. Ressel, Kids First, 84.

10. Ressel, Kids First, 85.

11. Christopher Kent, "Subluxation and Sudden Infant Death Syndrome," Chiropractic Leadership Alliance, 2021, https://insightcla.com/subluxation -and-sudden-infant-death-syndrome/; Christopher Kent, "Pediatric Chiropractic in the 21st Century," Chiropractic Leadership Alliance, 2021, https://insightcla.com/pediatric-chiropractic-in-the-21st-century/.

12. Dorte Bladt, "Babies and Chiropractic," *Get Ahead Kids* 5, no. 5 (September– October 2013).

13. A. Bonci and C. Wynne, "The Interface between Sudden Infant Death Syndrome and Chiropractic," *Journal of Chiropractic Research* 5, no. 3 (1989): 78; J. Stiga, "Sudden Infant Death Syndrome," *American Chiropractor*, October 1983, p. 28; B. D. Banks, R. W. Beck, M. Columbus, P. M. Gold, F. S. Kinsinger, and M. A. Lalonde, "Sudden Infant Death Syndrome: A Literature Review with Chiropractic Implications," *Journal of Manipulative and Physiological Therapeutics* 10, no. 5 (1987): 246.

Chapter 8

1. Terry L. Wahls, *Minding My Mitochondria: How I Overcame Secondary Progressive Multiple Sclerosis (MS) and Got out of My Wheelchair*, 2nd ed. (Iowa City, IA: TZ Press, 2010).

2. United States Environmental Protection Agency, "Basic Information about Mercury," December 21, 2021, https://www.epa.gov/mercury/basic-information -about-mercury.

3. Agency for Toxic Substances and Disease Registry, "Public Health Statement: Aluminum," September 2008, https://www.atsdr.cdc.gov/ToxProfiles/tp22 -c1-b.pdf; Katrin Klotz, Wobbeke Weistenhöfer, Frauke Neff, Andrea Hartwig, Christoph van Thriel, and Hans Drexler, "The Health Effects of Aluminum Exposure," *Deutsches Ärzteblatt* 114, no. 39 (2017), https://www.ncbi.nlm.nih .gov/pmc/articles/PMC5651828/.

4. Rachael Link, "12 Cilantro Benefits, Nutrition and Recipes," *Dr. Axe*, June 1, 2019, https://draxe.com/cilantro-benefits/. This article appears on the website of Dr. Josh Axe, a well-respected doctor of natural medicine, chiropractor, and clinical nutritionist. He is also the author of several books, including the

Amazon best seller *Eat Dirt: Why Leaky Gut May Be the Root Cause of Your Health Problems and 5 Surprising Steps to Cure It*. I highly recommend reading this and his other books.

5. Terry Wahls and Eve Adamson, *The Wahls Protocol: A Radical New Way to Treat All Chronic Autoimmune Conditions Using Paleo Principles* (New York: Avery, 2014).

6. Josh Axe, *Bone Broth Breakthrough* (n.p.: Axe Wellness, 2016).

7. Josh Axe, *Eat Dirt: Why Leaky Gut May Be the Root Cause of Your Health Problems and 5 Surprising Steps to Cure It* (New York: Harper Wave, 2016).

Chapter 9

1. Joseph Mercola, *Dark Deception: Discover the Truth about the Benefits of Sunlight Exposure* (Nashville, TN: Thomas Nelson, 2008).

2. American Academy of Dermatology Association, "Skin Cancer," June 1, 2021, https://www.aad.org/media/stats-skin-cancer.

3. Mercola, *Dark Deception*, 3.

4. Michael F. Holick, "Sunlight and Vitamin D for Bone Health and Prevention of Autoimmune Diseases, Cancers, and Cardiovascular Disease," *American Journal of Clinical Nutrition* 80 (December 2004): 1678S–1688S.

5. "Unraveling the Sun's Role in Depression," *WebMD*, December 5, 2002, https://www.webmd.com/mental-health/news/20021205/unraveling-suns-role-in-depression.

6. Mayo Clinic, "Antidepressants: Selecting One That's Right for You," December 31, 2019, https://www.mayoclinic.org/diseases-conditions/depression/in-depth/antidepressants/art-20046273.

7. Yanhping Lin, John L. Ubels, Mark P. Schotanus, Zhaohong Yin, Victorina Pintea, Bruce D. Hammock, and Mitchell A. Watsky, "Enhancement of Vitamin D Metabolites in the Eye Following Vitamin D3 Supplementation and UV-B Irradiation," *Current Eye Research* 37, no. 10 (October 2012): 871–878.

Chapter 10

1. Zig Ziglar, *Goals: How to Set Them, How to Reach Them*, read by Zig Ziglar (Nightingale Conant, 1989), audiobook.

2. Mayo Clinic, "Meditation: A Simple, Fast Way to Reduce Stress," May 5, 2014, https://www.mayoclinic.org/tests-procedures/meditation/in-depth/meditation/art-20045858.

3. Maamer Slimani, David Tod, Helmi Chaabene, Bianca Miarka, and Karim Chamari, "Effects of Mental Imagery on Muscular Strength in Healthy and Patient Participants: A Systematic Review," *Journal of Sports Science and Medicine* 15, no. 3 (September 2016): 434–450.

4. Brian C. Clark, Niladri K. Mahato, Masato Nakazawa, Timothy D. Law, and James S. Thomas, "The Power of the Mind: The Cortex as a Critical Determinant of Muscle Strength/Weakness," *Journal of Neurophysiology* 112, no. 12 (December 2014): 3219–3226.

5. A. Toth, Eoghan McNeill, Kevin Hayes, A. Moran, and M. Campbell, "Does Mental Practice Still Enhance Performance? A 24 Year Follow-Up and Meta-analytic Replication and Extension," *Psychology of Sport and Exercise* 48 (February 2020), https://doi.org/10.1016/j.psychsport.2020.101672.

6. Nicolò F. Bernardi, Matteo De Buglio, Pietro D. Trimarchi, Alfonso Chielli, and Emanuela Bricolo, "Mental Practice Promotes Motor Anticipation: Evidence from Skilled Music Performance," *Frontiers in Human Neuroscience* 7 (2013): 451.

7. Bernie Siegel, *Love, Medicine and Miracles: Lessons Learned about Self-Healing from a Surgeon's Experience with Exceptional Patients*, 60th ed. (New York: William Morrow, 2011).

8. Roger Collier, "Imagined Illnesses Can Cause Real Problems for Medical Students," *Canadian Medical Association Journal* 178, no. 7 (2008): 820.

9. Joe Dispenza, *Breaking the Habit of Being Yourself: How to Lose Your Mind and Create a New One* (New York: Hay House, 2012).

Chapter 12

1. Barbara Johnson, *Leaking Laffs between Pampers and Depends* (Nashville, TN: Thomas Nelson, 2000), 67.

2. Harvard T. H. Chan School of Public Health, "Vitamins and Minerals," *Nutrition Source*, accessed January 18, 2022, https://www.hsph.harvard.edu/nutritionsource/vitamins/.

3. Mayo Clinic, "Supplements: Nutrition in a Pill?," November 17, 2020, https://www.mayoclinic.org/healthy-lifestyle/nutrition-and-healthy-eating/in-depth/supplements/art-20044894.

4. Suruchi Mishra, Bryan Stierman, Jaime J. Gahche, and Nancy Potischman, "Dietary Supplement Use among Adults: United States, 2017–2018," National Center for Health Statistics Data Brief No. 399, February 2021, https://www.cdc.gov/nchs/products/databriefs/db399.htm.

5. Mari Carmen Gomez-Cabrera, Michael Ristow, and Jose Viña, "Antioxidant Supplements in Exercise: Worse Than Useless?," *American Journal of Physiology-Endocrinology and Metabolism* 302, no. 4 (February 2012): E476.

6. Steven H. Zeisel, "Antioxidants Suppress Apoptosis," *Journal of Nutrition* 134, no. 11 (November 2004): 3179S.

7. Royal Lee, "Recent Conclusions in Malnutrition," paper presented at the American Naprapathic Association Convention, Chicago, June 1943, https://www.seleneriverpress.com/images/pdfs/770_RECENT_CONCLUSIONS_IN_MALNUTRITION_by_ROYAL_LEE_1943_Reprint_30.pdf.

8. Royal Lee, *Lectures of Dr. Royal Lee*, vol. 2, ed. Mark R. Anderson and Stephanie S. Anderson (Fort Collins, CO: Selene River Press, n.d.), CDs.

9. Destiny Bezrutczyk, "What Are the Differences in Addiction between Men and Women?" Addiction Center, March 25, 2021, https://www.addictioncenter.com/addiction/differences-men-women/; "Food Addiction," PsychGuides.com, accessed January 20, 2022, https://www.psychguides.com/eating-disorder/.

10. "Abundance of Fructose Not Good for the Liver," *Harvard Health* (blog), September 2011, https://www.health.harvard.edu/heart-health/abundance-of-fructose-not-good-for-the-liver-heart.

11. Mark Hyman, "Fatty Liver Is More Dangerous Than You Might Realize: Here's How to Heal It," *Dr. Hyman* (blog), May 5, 2016, https://drhyman.com/blog/2016/05/05/fatty-liver-is-more-dangerous-than-you-might-realize-heres-how-to-heal-it/.

12. Jeffrey B. Schwimmer, Reena Deutsch, Tanaz Kahen, Joel E. Lavine, Christina Stanley, and Cynthia Behling, "Prevalence of Fatty Liver in Children and Adolescents," *Pediatrics* 118, no. 4 (October 2006): 1388–1393.

13. Rudy Mawer, "6 Reasons Why High-Fructose Corn Syrup Is Bad for You," *Healthline*, September 27, 2019, https://www.healthline.com/nutrition/why-high-fructose-corn-syrup-is-bad.

14. Jillian Kubala, "12 Common Foods with High Fructose Corn Syrup," *Healthline*, August 30, 2021, https://www.healthline.com/nutrition/20-foods-with-high-fructose-corn-syrup#section17.

Chapter 13

1. Johns Hopkins Medicine, "Keep Your Brain Young with Music," accessed January 20, 2022, https://www.hopkinsmedicine.org/health/wellness-and -prevention/keep-your-brain-young-with-music.

2. Anita Kar, "Musical Chills: Why They Give Us Thrills," *McGill Newsroom*, January 10, 2011, https://www.mcgill.ca/newsroom/channels/news/musical -chills-why-they-give-us-thrills-170538.

3. "The 500 Greatest Songs of All Time," *Rolling Stone*, September 15, 2021, https://www.rollingstone.com/music/music-lists/best-songs-of-all -time-1224767/.

Chapter 14

1. Erin Jackson, Robin Shoemaker, Nika Larian, and Lisa Cassis, "Adipose Tissue as a Site of Toxin Accumulation," *Comprehensive Physiology* 7, no. 4 (2017), https://www.ncbi.nlm.nih.gov/pmc/articles/PMC6101675/; J. L. Tang-Péronard, H. R. Andersen, T. K. Jensen, and B. L. Heitmann, "Endocrine-Disrupting Chemicals and Obesity Development in Humans: A Review," *Obesity Review* 12, no. 8 (August 2011), https://pubmed.ncbi.nlm.nih .gov/21457182/.

2. R. Meerman and A. J. Brown, "When Somebody Loses Weight, Where Does the Fat Go?," *BMJ*, December 16, 2014, http://dx.doi.org/10.1136/bmj.g7257.

Chapter 15

1. "Sleep and Longevity," *Doctor Oz Show*, accessed December 1, 2021, https:// www.drozshow.com/blog/sleep-and-longevity.

2. Zlatan Krizan and Anne D. Herlache, "Sleep Disruption and Aggression: Implications for Violence and Its Prevention," *Psychology of Violence* 6, no. 4 (October 2016): 542–552.

3. Poliquin editorial staff, "Practical Ways to Get Better Sleep," Poliquin Group, August 13, 2014, https://www.poliquinstore.com/articles/the-super-list-of -practical-ways-to-get-better-sleep/.

4. Zhilei Shan, Hongfei Ma, Manling Xie, Peipei Yan, Yanjun Guo, Wei Bao, Ying Rong, Chandra L. Jackson, Frank B. Hu, and Liegang Liu, "Sleep Duration and Risk of Type 2 Diabetes: A Meta-analysis of Prospective Studies," *Diabetes Care* 38, no. 3 (March 2015): 529–537.

5. Sami Ouanes and Julius Popp, "High Cortisol and the Risk of Dementia and Alzheimer's Disease: A Review of the Literature," *Frontiers in Aging Neuroscience*, March 1, 2019, https://doi.org/10.3389/fnagi.2019.00043.

6. E. Van Cauter, R. Leproult, and L. Plat, "Age-Related Changes in Slow Wave Sleep and REM Sleep and Relationship with Growth Hormone and Cortisol Levels in Healthy Men," *JAMA* 284, no. 7 (2000): 861–868.

7. Elsevier, "Rotating Night Shift Work Can Be Hazardous to Your Health," *ScienceDaily*, January 5, 2015, https://www.sciencedaily.com/releases/2015/01/150105081757.htm.

8. Matthew Walker, *Why We Sleep: Unlocking the Power of Sleep and Dreams* (New York: Scribner, 2017).

9. Walker, *Why We Sleep*.

10. Michigan Medicine, "Why Daylight Saving Time Could Increase Your Heart Attack Risk," *Michigan Health* (blog), March 8, 2017, https://healthblog.uofmhealth.org/heart-health/why-daylight-saving-time-could-increase-your-heart-attack-risk.

11. Carla S. Möller-Levet, Simon N. Archer, Giselda Bucca, Emma E. Laing, Ana Slak, Renata Kabiljo, June C. Y. Lo, Nayantara Santhi, Malcolm von Schantz, Colin P. Smith, and Derk-Jan Dijk, "Effects of Insufficient Sleep on Circadian Rhythmicity and Expression Amplitude of the Human Blood Transcriptome," *Proceedings of the National Academy of Sciences of the United States of America* 110, no. 12 (2013), https://doi.org/10.1073/pnas.1217154110; Elsevier, "Rotating Night Shift Work."

12. Phyllis C. Zee and Fred W. Turek, "Everywhere and in Both Directions," *Archives of Internal Medicine* 166, no. 16 (2006): 1686–1688; M. R. Irwin, A. Mascovich, J. C. Gillin, R. Willoughby, J. Pike, and T. L. Smith, "Partial Sleep Deprivation Reduces Natural Killer Cell Activity in Humans," *Psychosomatic Medicine* 56, vol. 6 (1994): 493–498; Elsevier, "Rotating Night Shift Work."

13. H. P. Van Dongen, G. Maislin, J. M. Mullington, and D. F. Dinges, "The Cumulative Cost of Additional Wakefulness: Dose-Response Effects on Neurobehavioral Functions and Sleep Physiology from Chronic Sleep Restriction and Total Sleep Deprivation," *Sleep* 26, no. 2 (2003): 117.

14. Van Dongen et al., "The Cumulative Cost of Additional Wakefulness," 117.

15. Chris Obenschain, "Got 60 Minutes for a Nap? How About 6?," *WebMD*, accessed December 15, 2021, https://www.webmd.com/sleep-disorders/features/got-60-minutes-for-a-nap-how-about-6#1.

16. Rob Faigin, *Natural Hormonal Enhancement: The Ultimate Strategy for Lifetime Youthfulness, Physique Transformation, and Super-Health* (Cedar Mountain, NC: Extique, 2000).

17. Walker, *Why We Sleep.*

18. J. F. Pagel and Bennett L. Parnes, "Medications for the Treatment of Sleep Disorders: An Overview," *Primary Care Companion to the Journal of Clinical Psychiatry* 3, no. 3 (June 2001): 118–125.

19. James L. Oschman, "Can Electrons Act as Antioxidants? A Review and Commentary," *Journal of Alternative Complementary Medicine* 13, no. 9 (November 2007): 955–967.

20. The conference was the Chiropractic Leadership Alliance's "Leadership Summit," held in Chicago on October 24, 2008.

21. Denise Mann, "Negative Ions Create Positive Vibes: There's Something in the Air That Just May Boost Your Mood—Get a Whiff of Negative Ions," *WebMD*, May 6, 2002, https://www.webmd.com/balance/features/negative-ions-create-positive-vibes.

22. Walker, *Why We Sleep.*

Chapter 16

1. Centers for Medicare and Medicaid Services, "Table 01: National Health Expenditures and Selected Economic Indicators, Levels and Annual Percent Change: Calendar Years 2012–2028," accessed January 9, 2022, https://www.cms.gov/Research-Statistics-Data-and-Systems/Statistics-Trends-and-Reports/NationalHealthExpendData/NationalHealthAccountsProjected.html.

2. Colin Schultz, "Doctors Warned Life Expectancy Could Go Down, and It Did," *Smithsonian*, September 21, 2012, http://www.smithsonianmag.com/smart-news/doctors-warned-life-expectancy-could-go-down-and-it-did-45735996/?no-ist.

3. Daniel J. DeNoon, "U.S. Life Expectancy Down," *WebMD*, December 9, 2010, http://www.webmd.com/healthy-aging/news/20101209/us-life-expectancy-down.

4. David S. Freedman, "Obesity—United States, 1988–2008," *Morbidity and Mortality Weekly Report*, January 14, 2011, https://www.cdc.gov/mmwr/preview/mmwrhtml/su6001a15.htm.

5. Centers for Disease Control and Prevention, "Diabetes Report Card 2012," 2012, http://www.cdc.gov/diabetes/pubs/pdf/diabetesreportcard.pdf.

6. R. Morgan Griffin, "10 Health Problems Related to Stress That You Can Fix," *WebMD*, April 1, 2014, http://www.webmd.com/balance/stress-management/features/10-fixable-stress-related-health-problems.

7. West Hartford Chiropractic, "New Evidence Supports the Safety of Chiropractic Care," accessed January 9, 2022, https://westhartfordchiropractic.com/press-release/new-evidence-supports-the-safety-of-chiropractic-care.html.

8. Clayton J. Campbell, Christopher Kent, Arthur Banne, Amir Amiri, and Ronald W. Pero, "Surrogate Indication of DNA Repair in Serum after Long Term Chiropractic Intervention: A Retrospective Study," *Journal of Vertebral Subluxation Research*, February 18, 2005, pp. 1–5.

9. Connie Lauerman, "New Respect Boosts Chiropractic as a Mainstream Therapy," *Chicago Tribune*, November 26, 2000, p. 401.

10. Christopher Kent, "Medicare Folly," Chiropractic Leadership Alliance, accessed January 20, 2022, https://insightcla.com/medicare-folly/.

11. John F. Kennedy, inaugural address, January 20, 1961, Washington, DC, https://avalon.law.yale.edu/20th_century/kennedy.asp.

12. Ralph Waldo Emerson, *The Conduct of Life* (Cambridge, MA: Houghton, Mifflin, 1883), 49.

Appendix

1. C. Kent, "Models of Vertebral Subluxation: A Review," *Journal of Vertebral Subluxation Research* 1, no. 1 (August 1996): 1–7.

2. P. C. Brennan, J. J. Triano, M. McGregor, K. Kokjohn, M. A. Hondras, and D. C. Brennan, "Enhanced Neutrophil Respiratory Burst as a Biological Marker for Manipulation Forces: Duration of the Effect and Association with Substance P and Tumor Necrosis Factor," *Journal of Manipulative and Physiological Therapeutics* 15, no. 2 (1992): 83.

3. Jeffrey L. Selano, Brett C. Hightower, Bruce Pfleger, Karen Freeley Collins, and John D. Grostic, "The Effects of Specific Upper Cervical Adjustments on the DC4 Counts of HIV Positive Patients," *Chiropractic Research Journal* 3, no. 1 (1994): 32.

Index

circadian rhythm, 183–186
and exercise, 145–146
birth, subluxations during, 98,
    108–109, 110
blood flow, 73
blood pressure, 81, 100–101
blood sugar levels, 82, 160
blood vessels, 72–73
body
    communication between brain
        and, 93–94, 109
    innate intelligence of, 53–58, 66
body fat, loss of, 178–179
bone broth, 120
bone spurs, 212
brain
    and circulatory system, 72–73
    communication between body
        and, 93–94, 109
    and digestive process, 88–89
    Dr. Watson's story, 94–100
    importance of, in body, 69–70
    and nervous system, 68–71
    and spinal column, 86–88
breathing
    effect of stress on, 172–174
    exercises for, 175–179
    mechanics of, 172
    overview of, 171–172
    rhythm of, 174–175, 176–179
burns from sun exposure, 124–125
Bush, Zack, 147

C
cadmium poisoning, 116
cancer
    antioxidants and apoptosis, 157
    cigarette smoking and, 40–41
    early detection of, 100
    effect of visualization on, 139
    lifestyle and, 64–65
    music and, 166–168

prevention of, 63, 64
relationship between genes and envi-
    ronment in, 51–53, 60–62
role of healthy lifestyle in over-
    coming, 14–15
and sunlight exposure, 124–125
Candida albicans, 30
car accidents, subluxations caused by, 108
cavities, 209–210
CD4 cells (T-lymphocytes), 214
cells
    antioxidants and apoptosis, 157
    environment of, and DNA, 59–60
    innate intelligence of, 53–58
    replacement of, 89
Centers for Disease Control and
    Prevention (CDC), 25, 199
charcoal, detoxifying properties of, 120
chemical stress. *See also* toxicity
    lifestyle modifications, 101
    overview of, 39–41
    preventing deficiency, 151
    wellness and, 42–44
chemistry of music, 168–170
Chestnut, James, 24, 66
chicken pox, 35
children
    fatty liver in, 161–162
    and innate intelligence of body, 56, 57
    lifestyle/preventable diseases in, 25, 198
    subluxations during childhood,
        108–111
chiropractic care
    Dan's story, 105–108
    Dr. Watson's story, 94–100
    focus of evaluation in, 103–104
    getting, on regular basis, 111, 208–209
    health benefits of, xii–xiv, 99–101, 107,
        111, 201–202
    Javad Rashidian's story, x–xiv
    for newborns, 109, 110–111
    overview of, 205–211
    reducing blood pressure with, 101
    specific nature of adjustment, 207–208

subluxation models, 211–215
subluxations simplified, 215–216
chlorine, toxicity of, 118
choices and quality of life, 15–17
cholesterol levels, 81, 100–101,
    129, 159, 160
cholesterol medication for children, 25
cigarette smoking, 40–41
cilantro, 119
circadian rhythm, 183–186
circulatory system, 72–73, 81
civil rights movement, 197
Civil War, 197
clay, detoxifying properties of, 120
cognitive performance, sleep depriva-
    tion and, 189
cold weather, as stressor, 29
coordination
    effect of visualization on, 138
    three-minute workouts focused on, 146
core values
    alignment of, with priorities, 148–149
    determining, 45–49
cortisol, 81, 82, 129, 159, 183, 187
coughing and innate intelligence of
    body, 57
cravings
    during pregnancy, 56
    stress-related, 159–161

D

daily life, incorporating movement
    into, 144–148
dance, 167–168, 169
Dark Deception (Mercola), 124,
    125, 126, 128
daylight saving time, 188
deep breathing, 176–179
degeneration, 106–107, 212
dentistry, 206–207, 209–210
depression, 127, 186–188
detoxification, 118–121, 177–179

diabetes, 63, 64, 82, 100, 183, 199
diaphragmatic breathing, 172, 175–176
diarrhea, 57
diet
    how to eat, 78–79, 159–163
    increasing melatonin in body, 185–186
    nutrition and supplements, 152–159
    overview of, 151–152
dietary fat, 198–199
digestion, 74–75, 81, 88–89
digital inclinometry, 104
diseases. See illness
Dispenza, Joe, 141
DNA and environment, 58–63, 68–69
dopamine, 168–169
Doyle, Arthur Conan, 67
dreams
    aspirations, 1–2, 5–6, 18–19, 35,
        132, 138, 200
    in sleep, 140, 192
Dyer, Wayne, 134
dysafferentation, 213
dyskenesia (pathomechanics), 211–212

E

early detection of disease, 100, 201
earthing, 192
Eat Dirt (Axe), 120
eating habits, 78–79, 159–163.
    See also diet
Ebola, 30–31
Edison, Thomas, 1
Einstein, Albert, 21, 37, 143
electroencephalogram, 96–97
electromyography, 104
embarrassment, reaction of brain to, 72
Emerson, Ralph Waldo, 204
emotional stress, 41–42, 77
emotions
    and autonomic responses, 75
    as motivation to move, 149–150
    sleep deprivation and stability of,
        186–188

power of visualization for dealing with, 135–141
wellness and, 42–44

About the Author

AMIR A. RASHIDIAN holds bachelor of science degrees in chemistry and human biology and a doctorate in chiropractic. He is the founder of the Mid Atlantic Chiropractic Center. Established in 2006 and hosting more than twenty thousand patient visits annually, the Mid Atlantic Chiropractic Center focuses on high-tech diagnostics to detect and correct disturbances in the nervous system. The doctors at the center promote drugless health solutions, working with patients to eliminate the causes of disease rather than merely suppress the symptoms.

As a consultant, Dr. Rashidian has worked with eighteen chiropractic practices, sixteen of which were start-up businesses that all reached profitability within the first three months of launch. He also has opened three very successful chiropractic practices.

An active speaker at corporate events, conventions, and churches, Dr. Rashidian is also frequently interviewed by local TV, radio, and newspaper outlets, as well as for podcasts. Additionally, he serves on the board of directors of Habitat for Humanity of Frederick County and is a major financial supporter of its local building projects. He also serves as the chairman of the elder leadership team at Grace Community Church in Frederick, Maryland. He has won multiple honors and awards, including Business Leader of the Year from Frederick Community College and Philanthropist of the Year from Habitat for Humanity.

He married his sweetheart, Brandi, in 2005, and they have three sons. No stranger to stress, Dr. Rashidian has made it his mission to help create a healthier next generation by improving the lives of children and families today.